AF291969

A First Introduction to Science

ENCYCLOPEDIA of LEARNING

DISCOVER SCIENCE

LIGHT
SOUND & MOTION

& ELECTRICITY
& MAGNETISM

Predominant artwork & imagery source:
Shutterstock.com

Copyright: North Parade Publishing Ltd.

3-6 Henrietta Mews,

Bath,

BA2 6LR, UK

First Published: 2019

Printed in China.

SCIENCE
Contents

LIGHT SOUND & MOTION
Contents

ELECTRICITY & MAGNETISM
Contents

A First Introduction to Science

ENCYCLOPEDIA of LEARNING

DISCOVER
SCIENCE

Matter

Matter is a substance that has mass and occupies space. Everything you find around you is made up of matter. We can see, touch and interact with matter and all matter is made up of atoms. Matter can trap energy and release it in a different form.

States of Matter

Matter is found throughout the Universe. The physical state of molecules and atoms is known as the state of matter. Scientists are trying to understand more about matter, and learn about new states in which matter can exist.

On Earth, matter exists in these three common states:

1. Solid: The molecules that make up a solid substance are packed tightly together and are unable to move around freely. Solids have a definite shape and volume.

2. Liquid: In a liquid, the molecules of the substance are not packed too tightly. They have definite volume but do not have a definite shape. They simply take the shape of the container into which they are poured.

3. Gas: A gas is a form of matter in which there is a lot of space between the individual molecules. When you fill a container with a gas, it will expand to fit the container. If a gas is not confined, it will spread indefinitely.

▼ *Everything around us is made up of matter and all matter is made up of atoms.*

Solid: The atoms of a solid are packed closely together and form a definite shape.

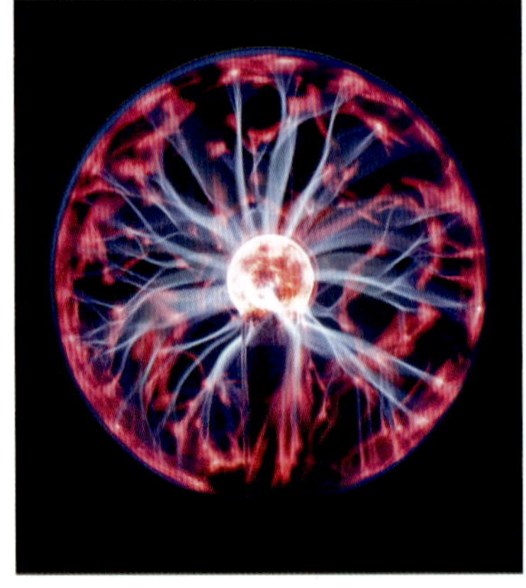

Do you Know?

Plasma and Bose-Einstein Condensate are two additional states of matter that exist on Earth only under special conditions.

Matter can change state

Did you know that matter can change from one form to another while remaining the same substance? The transformation of matter from one state into another is called phase change.

Let's see what water can teach us about the different states of matter. A glass of water is in liquid phase. Pour the water into an ice tray and leave it to cool in the fridge for a while. You'll notice that the water has turned into hard ice cubes! Water, as ice, is now in solid phase. If we do the opposite and heat the water, it will turn into water vapour. Now, water is in a gaseous phase!

Solids, liquids and gases can convert into any other form under suitable conditions. A solid can be melted into liquid when heat is applied, while freezing can convert a liquid into a solid. Boiling causes a liquid to turn into gas and condensation, a type of cooling, converts a gas into a liquid.

Fact File

We have all three states of matter inside our body at any given time! Our lungs are filled with air (a mixture of gases), our blood is liquid, and our bones, nerves, muscles, and organs are all solids!

► *When a star explodes, it creates the environment for a new star and planets to form.*

Gas: The atoms of a gas are not attracted to each other and spread out.

Stars and Matter

Stars are made up of lots of matter. At the end of its lifespan, a star explodes, releasing clouds of dust. Over a period of billions of years, the dust comes together to form stars and planets. Our planet, Earth, was formed by a similar process!

Liquid: The atoms of a liquid are loosely attracted to each other and don't have a shape.

Atoms and Molecules

Atoms are the basic building blocks of all the matter in the Universe. The name 'atom' is derived from the Greek word 'atomos', which means 'indivisible'. For a long time it was believed that atoms were the most basic particles and that there could not be anything smaller, but now we know that each atom has a nucleus and electrons. Atoms combine with other atoms to form molecules.

Peering into an Atom

An atom has a nucleus at its centre, which is made up of protons and neutrons. Protons have positive charge while neutrons carry no charge. Surrounding this nucleus, like a cloud, are the negatively charged electrons. Since positive and negative charges attract each other, the electrons don't fly away!

To better visualise the structure of an atom, think of the Sun as the nucleus, and the planets revolving around the Sun, as the electrons.

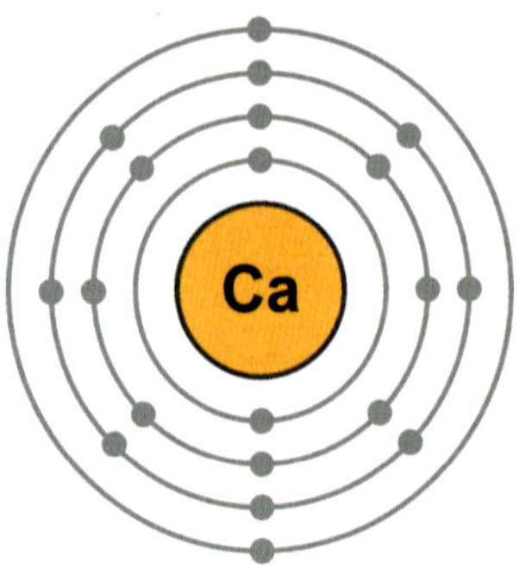

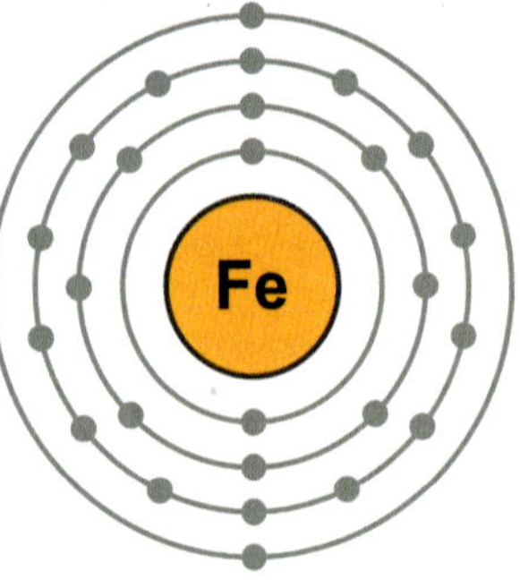

Atomic Number and Mass

The number of protons in the nucleus of an atom is called the atomic number. The atomic number is what makes one element different from another. The element calcium, which has an atomic number of 20, is very different from iron, which has an atomic number of 26. The number of protons and neutrons in the nucleus of an atom is referred to as the atomic mass or atomic weight.

Size of Atoms

An atom is very small. It is difficult even to imagine how tiny it is. Look at the thickness of a strand of hair – it is really small, isn't it? On average, an atom is about a million times smaller than this!

In order to view atoms, scientists use very powerful and complex microscopes that use electrons instead of light rays. These electron beams pick up tiny details and allow us to view things a million times larger than they actually are.

▶ *A powerful electron microscope can enable us to view individual molecules and atoms.*

Atoms form Elements

Atoms make up the most basic substances, which are called elements. These elements are made up of atoms of the same kind and they act as building blocks for all kinds of matter.

Let's take a bar of pure gold. The entire bar is made up of only gold atoms. No ordinary chemical processes can convert this bar of gold (or any other element) into simpler substances.

▲ *A bar of gold is made up of only gold atoms and nothing else.*

Molecules

Atoms don't usually exist alone, but combine together. The combination of two or more atoms is called a molecule.

Do you know how atoms combine? The outermost part of the atoms share electrons to bond together. Two different atoms with unique properties combine to form a molecule that is very different. When a lightweight metal, such as sodium, and a greenish, poisonous gas called chlorine combine, they form salt, a substance that we use every day!

Molecules come in different sizes. A molecule of oxygen has only two atoms, while others like plastic or wood are made up of millions of atoms linked together.

▲ *The protons and neutrons are concentrated in the middle of an atom, referred to as the nucleus.*

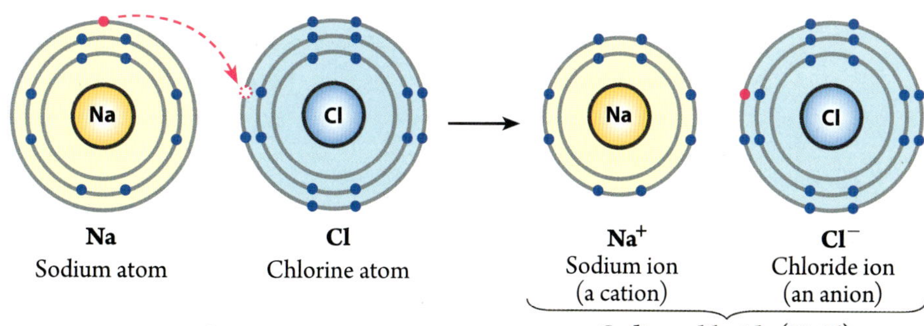

Na
Sodium atom

Cl
Chlorine atom

Na$^+$
Sodium ion
(a cation)

Cl$^-$
Chloride ion
(an anion)

Sodium chloride (NaCl)

Solids and Liquids

Solids are made up of atoms and molecules that stay fixed in place. They don't move around, nor do they get closer or farther from each other. Solids have a fixed structure and are difficult to change unless a lot of force is applied. There are solids that are soft and flexible and can break apart easily. Unlike solids, liquids have atoms and molecules that are free to move around and change shape.

Solids

Solids have tightly packed atoms arranged in specific rigid patterns. You need to apply force to break apart a solid. Look around you and you'll spot many solids, ranging from the bricks and wood that make up your home, to vehicles and machines made up of heavy-duty, sturdy solid materials.

Solids come in different types. Some are hard, some are smooth and some are crystals. Ever wondered what makes one solid heavier than another? A solid's mass depends on the structure of its atoms. For example, if a solid is made up of tightly packed, heavy atoms that weigh more and are difficult to break apart, the solid itself will be heavy and difficult to break apart.

Solids come in many textures, shapes, colours and properties. Let's look at a few kinds of solids:

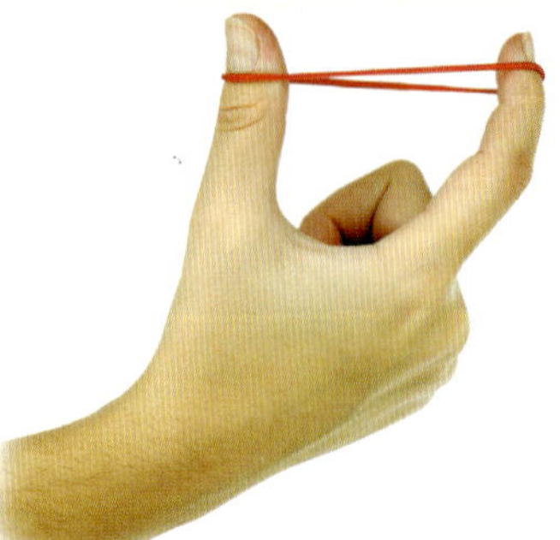

Crystal	Fibres	Elastic
They have sharp corners and straight edges. Quartz and diamond are crystals.	Long, thin and flexible strands that, when woven together, can form strong fabrics. Jute and hemp are fibres.	Can stretch and return to its original shape after a force is applied. Rubber is a good example of this.

Fact File

Graphene aerogel is the lightest solid ever produced. It is made up of carbon atoms and it has a lot of empty space between the atoms. It is seven times lighter than air!

▲ Different liquids have varying viscosity – honey is more viscous and slower to flow than milk.

Liquids

The distance between the particles of a liquid cannot be altered. Liquids can either be pure and made up of the same molecules throughout or be a mixture of different substances. Sometimes it is difficult to see or guess that a liquid is actually a mixture! Milk, for example, is an emulsion of water molecules mixed with fat, protein and lactose (milk sugar)!

Liquids also vary in thickness. A thick liquid is said to be 'viscous' and will flow more slowly than a liquid that is watery. Water, for example, is less viscous compared to honey or tar, which are both very thick in consistency.

◄ A rock embedded with purple amethyst crystals is an example of a crystalline solid.

Lightweight	Heavy
Some solids, like Styrofoam, are made up of 98% air and repeating units of carbon and hydrogen (two lightweight atoms).	Rocks and stones such as basalt or granite are made up of heavy atoms closely packed together. This is what makes them heavy.

Did you know?

When we think of metals, we imagine them as solids. However, the metal mercury exists as a liquid at room temperature! Mercury is a shiny, metallic liquid that forms thick blobs when dropped.

Types of Gases

The air we breathe is a mixture of different gases. Gases are all around us, yet we cannot see them. This is because, just like liquids, gases have no shape of their own. Inside a container, a gas will fill up the space by expanding its atoms and molecules. If left outside, a gas will continue to expand and its molecules drift apart.

Gases

There are different types of gases. Pure gases are made up of a single type of atom. Neon gas is a good example of this. Elemental gases are those like oxygen, nitrogen and hydrogen that are made up of atoms of the same element and remain stable under standard temperature and pressure.

Compound gases are made up of different atoms combined together. Carbon dioxide is a compound gas. Noble gases include helium, xenon, argon, neon, radon, krypton and oganesson. These gases are very stable and rarely ever react with other elements.

The atoms and molecules in a gas are not strongly linked to each other. They are free to move around, bump into one another and the sides of their container.

► *Deep sea divers carry air cylinders to enable them to breathe when underwater.*

Fact File

Despite its name, laughing gas (N_2O) does not induce laughter. Instead, when inhaled, it acts on the brain and makes you feel very happy and relaxed in just 3 minutes! N_2O is administered by dentists and doctors, for pain relief.

▲ *We breathe in oxygen and breathe out carbon dioxide through our lungs.*

Air

We need air to live. Air is present in the Earth's atmosphere and it is a mixture of gases that cover the Earth. Plants, animals and many other organisms depend on the air to survive.

Other gases like water vapour, carbon dioxide, hydrogen, ozone and methane are also found in the air in very small quantities. We survive by breathing in the oxygen from the air. Unlike us, plants require nitrogen and carbon dioxide to survive.

Air is also very special because it acts as a protective layer. It makes sure that the Earth does not become too warm or too cold. Meteoroids from space burn up in the air before they strike the Earth and are rendered harmless. Ozone is the name of the gas that blocks harmful rays from the Sun.

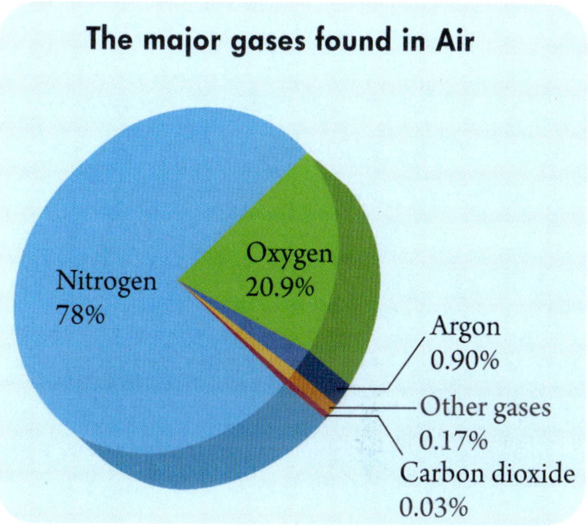

Greenhouse Gases

Greenhouse gases let in the sunlight into the atmosphere, but they trap heat, which increases the heat in the atmosphere. If there were no greenhouse gases, all the heat from the Sun would escape into space and Earth would be too cold for life to exist. Some greenhouse gases are found naturally, while others are released as a result of emissions from vehicles and other human activity. Carbon dioxide, water vapour and methane are greenhouse gases that naturally occur in the atmosphere.

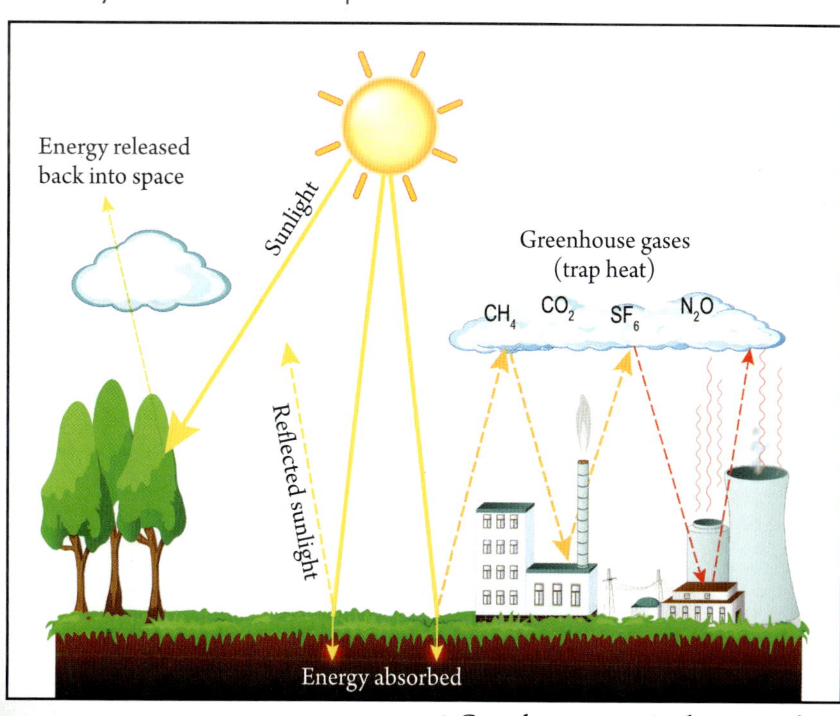

▲ *Greenhouse gases in the atmosphere trap heat from escaping.*

Periodic Table

Elements are chemical substances in their purest possible forms. All the atoms that make up an element are the same. To date, we know of more than 100 elements. Some elements are very rare while others are present all around us, and we use them every day! Two or more chemical elements can combine through strong or weak bonds to form compounds.

◄ *Dmitri Mendeleev came up with the idea of classifying elements based on their properties.*

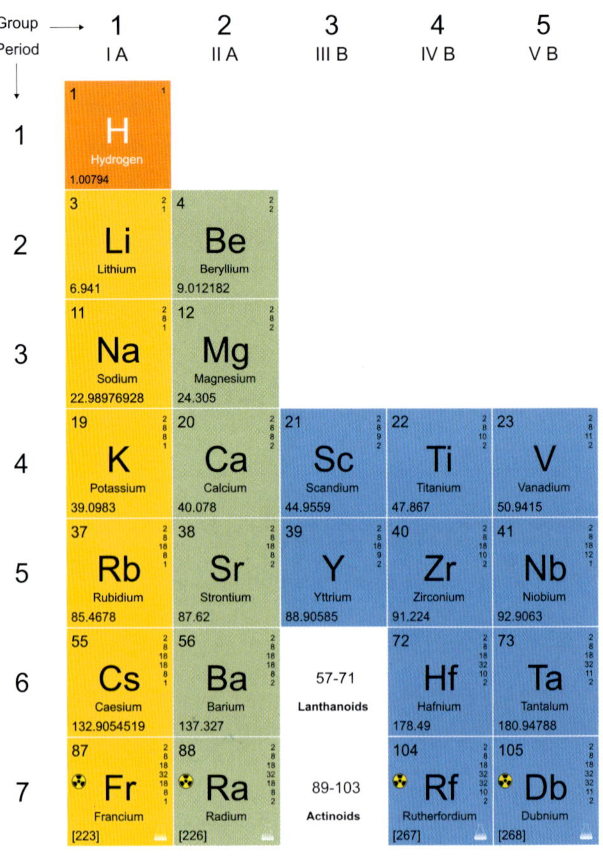

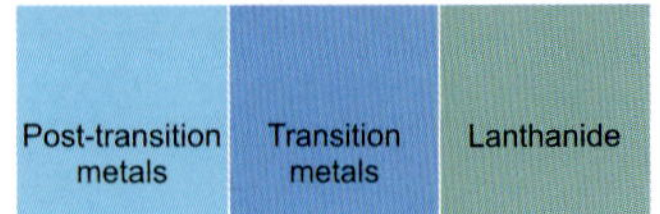

Periodic Table

The periodic table was invented by Dmitri Mendeleev, a Russian chemist, who came up with the idea of representing all of the elements in one table. He developed his idea in 1869. At that time, there were only 56 known elements. Mendeleev correctly predicted the properties of many undiscovered elements in the table. This table became commonly known as the Periodic table.

What the Table Shows Us

The table lists all the 118 elements that we know. In a periodic table, the rows of elements are called periods and the columns are called groups. There are 7 periods and 18 groups in total.

The table is very useful in providing important data about elements, such as:

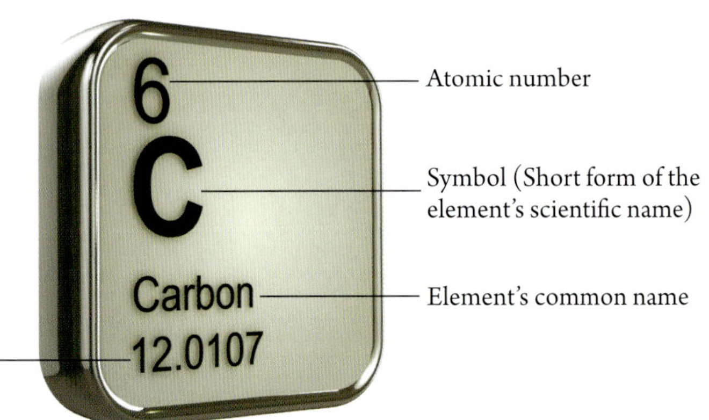

Atomic weight (also called the mass number)

6	7	8	9	10	11	12	13	14	15	16	17	18
VI B	VII B	VIII B	VIII B	VIII B	I B	II B	III A	IV A	V A	VI A	VII A	VIII A

												2 He Helium 4.002602
							5 B Boron 10.811	6 C Carbon 12.0107	7 N Nitrogen 14.0067	8 O Oxygen 15.9994	9 F Fluorine 18.9984032	10 Ne Neon 20.1797
							13 Al Aluminium 26.9815386	14 Si Silicon 28.0855	15 P Phosphorus 30.973762	16 S Sulfur 32.065	17 Cl Chlorine 35.453	18 Ar Argon 39.948
24 Cr Chromium 51.9961	25 Mn Manganese 54.938045	26 Fe Iron 55.845	27 Co Cobalt 58.933195	28 Ni Nickel 58.6934	29 Cu Copper 63.546	30 Zn Zinc 65.38	31 Ga Gallium 69.729	32 Ge Germanium 72.64	33 As Arsenic 74.9216	34 Se Selenium 78.96	35 Br Bromine 79.904	36 Kr Krypton 83.798
42 Mo Molybdenum 95.96	43 Tc Technetium [98]	44 Ru Ruthenium 101.07	45 Rh Rhodium 102.9055	46 Pd Palladium 106.42	47 Ag Silver 107.8682	48 Cd Cadmium 112.411	49 In Indium 114.818	50 Sn Tin 118.71	51 Sb Antimony 121.76	52 Te Tellurium 127.6	53 I Iodine 126.90447	54 Xe Xenon 131.293
74 W Tungsten 183.84	75 Re Rhenium 186.207	76 Os Osmium 190.23	77 Ir Iridium 192.217	78 Pt Platinum 195.084	79 Au Gold 196.966569	80 Hg Mercury 200.59	81 Tl Thallium 204.3833	82 Pb Lead 207.2	83 Bi Bismuth 208.9804	84 Po Polonium [209]	85 At Astatine [210]	86 Rn Radon [222]
106 Sg Seaborgium [271]	107 Bh Bohrium [272]	108 Hs Hassium [270]	109 Mt Meitnerium [276]	110 Ds Darmstadtium [281]	111 Rg Roentgenium [280]	112 Cn Copernicium [285]	113 Uut Ununtrium [286]	114 Fl Flerovium [289]	115 Uup Ununpentium [288]	116 Lv Livermorium [293]	117 Uus Ununseptium [294]	118 Uuo Ununoctium [294]

60 Nd Deodymium 144.242	61 Pm Promethium [145]	62 Sm Samarium 150.36	63 Eu Europium 151.964	64 Gd Gadolinium 157.25	65 Tb Terbium 158.9253	66 Dy Dysprosium 162.5	67 Ho Holmium 164.93032	68 Er Erbium 167.259	69 Tm Thulium 168.93421	70 Yb Ytterbium 173.054	71 Lu Lutetium 174.9668
92 U Uranium 238.02891	93 Np Neptunium [237]	94 Pu Plutonium [244]	95 Am Americium [243]	96 Cm Curium [247]	97 Bk Berkelium [247]	98 Cf Californium [251]	99 Es Einsteinium [252]	100 Fm Fermium [257]	101 Md Mendelevium [258]	102 No Nobelium [262]	103 Lr Lawrencium [262]

Uses of the Periodic Table

The elements arranged in the table can help to:

1) Predict the properties of different elements

2) Study the relationship between the elements

3) Keep track of and add newly discovered or synthesised elements

4) Examine the chemical behaviour of elements when they interact with each other

Fact File

Amongst the elements in the periodic table, carbon is thought to be the most unique because of its ability to form up to 10 million different compounds!

Solutions and Solvents, Acids and Bases

Some liquids, like water, have the ability to dissolve solids. Add a spoon of salt to water and, like magic, it looks as if the salt has disappeared! What has actually happened, however, is that the molecules of salt were pulled in different directions by the water molecules. We call this a solution. The solid that was dissolved is the solute and the water is the solvent.

Solutions can be diluted or concentrated, depending upon the number of solute particles that are dissolved in the solvent.

What is Saturation?

A solution allows solute particles to be added until there is no more space left between the solvent molecules. When this happens, the solute will no longer dissolve and instead will remain as a solid. Such a solution is said to be saturated. It has taken the maximum amount of solute particles possible. Heating might help to dissolve more solute particles, but when the solvent is cooled back down, the solute particles cannot remain dissolved and will form crystals.

▲ *An antacid dissolves in water and is consumed to counter acidity.*

◄ *A stain remover is a type of solvent used for dissolving tough stains on surfaces.*

Solvents We Use

Water is easily the most commonly used solvent on Earth! Other solvents that we often use include hand cleansers that can break up and dissolve dirt and germs, nail polish remover that can dissolve nail colour, stain removers that contain different solvents capable of getting rid of dirt, and spirit that removes paint stains and grease.

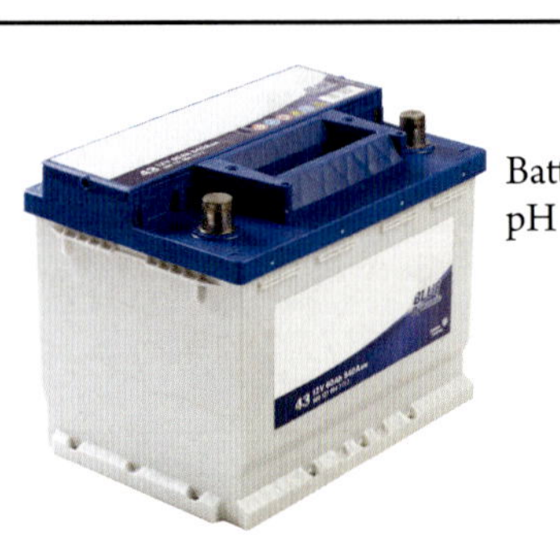

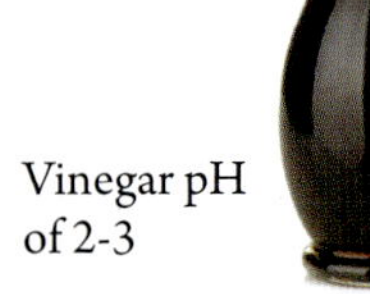

▲ *Solvents are essential for clearing up oil spills in the sea.*

Solvents Save The Day!

Have you tried dropping oil into water? You might have noticed that oil does not mix or dissolve in water. An oil spill at sea behaves similarly. This is a serious environmental problem, because spilled oil can cause widespread pollution and kill many types of wildlife, in and around the water.

Chemical substances called solvents can help disperse the oil into smaller, more manageable blobs that spread out and float away. This way, the oil is less likely to cause any significant harm.

Acids and Bases

Almost all liquids are either acids or bases. Scientists have classified acids and bases based on their properties. Acids are usually sour, while bases are bitter. Strong acids and bases are very dangerous, but are safer in their weaker forms, and can even be consumed! Vinegar is a good example of an edible acid, while baking soda is a base we use in baking. Antacids are also a base that we can consume as they are effective at treating indigestion.

How do we know whether an acid or base is strong or weak? We use what is called a pH scale. The scale has values from 1 to 14. Acids have pH under 7, with the strongest acids starting at 1. Bases have pH above 7. The strongest bases will have a pH value close to 14. A neutral solution has a pH of 7.

Fact File

Pure water is neutral, so it will have a pH value that is very close to 7!

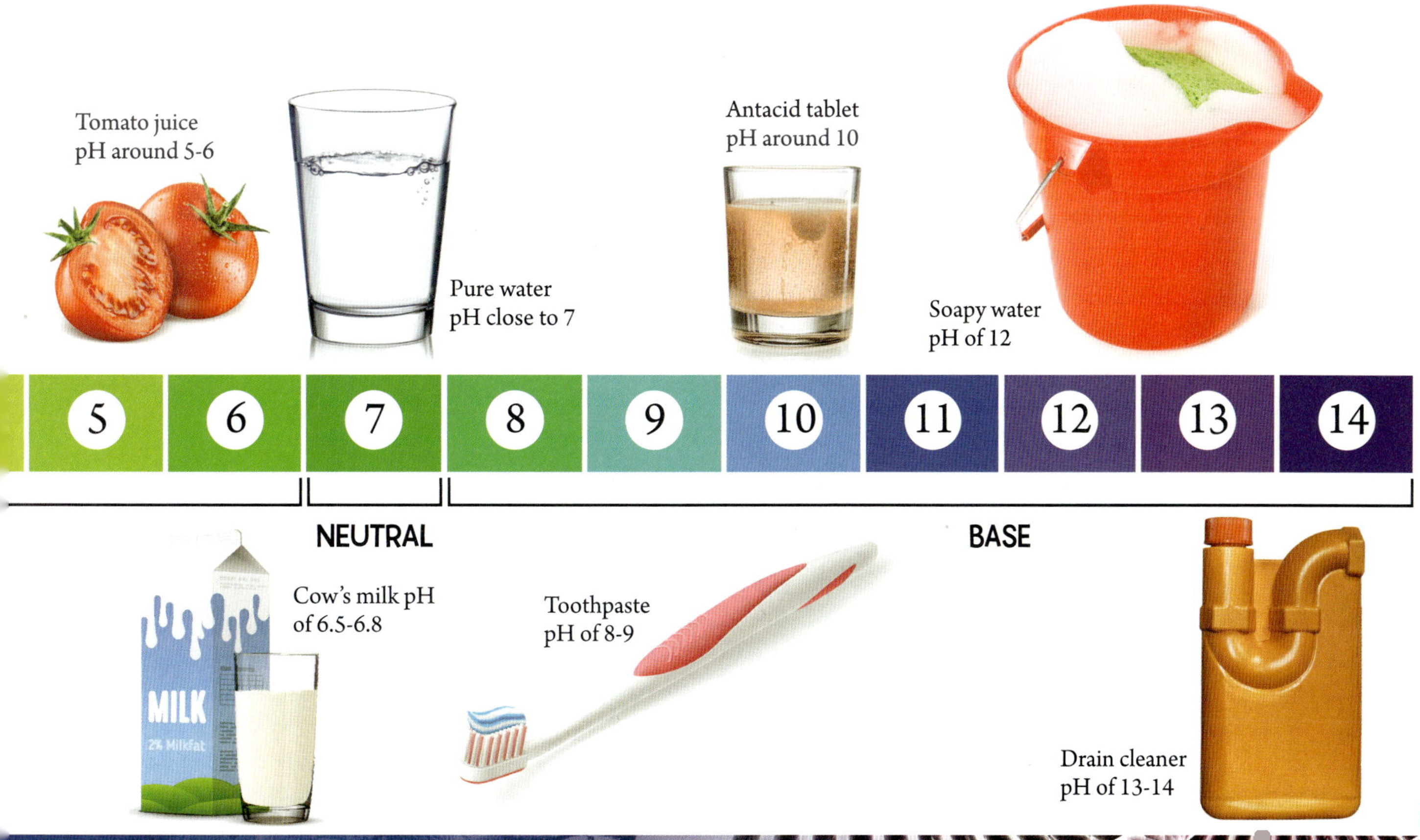

Tomato juice
pH around 5-6

Pure water
pH close to 7

Antacid tablet
pH around 10

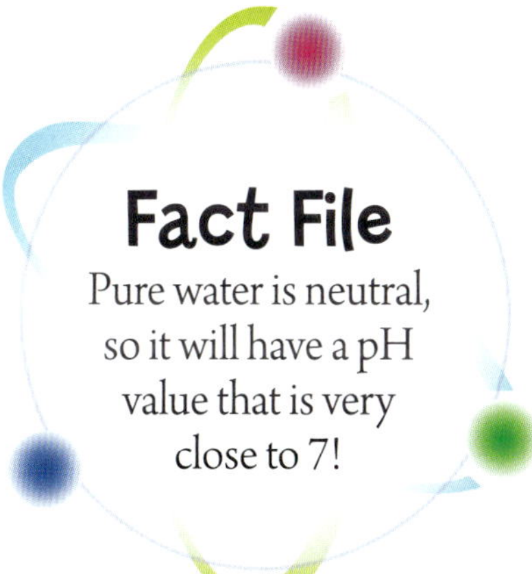

Soapy water
pH of 12

| 5 | 6 | 7 | 8 | 9 | 10 | 11 | 12 | 13 | 14 |

NEUTRAL

BASE

Cow's milk pH of 6.5-6.8

Toothpaste pH of 8-9

Drain cleaner pH of 13-14

Organic Chemistry

The study of carbon compounds is called organic chemistry. The element, carbon, combines with other elements such as hydrogen, nitrogen, and oxygen, to form different compounds. These organic compounds are the building blocks of all living things on Earth and they also form the basis of many important substances that we use everyday, such as plastics, medicines and petroleum.

Carbon Cycle

Living organisms need carbon for their survival. Although about 20 percent of living things are made up of carbon, there is only a limited amount of carbon present on Earth. How then is it possible for life to continue?

The answer is the carbon cycle!

This process allows carbon to be recycled continuously. Dead plants and animals decay naturally and release carbon dioxide (CO_2). Plants and trees use carbon dioxide and sunlight to grow. These, in turn, become food for animals. Animals grow and gain energy throughout their lives. They breathe out carbon dioxide that is again used by plants and animals. This is a continuous cycle. In this way, carbon is always made available.

The carbon cycle occurs in the oceans as well. In fact, they play a very important role. The oceans have 50 times more carbon than in the atmosphere. Carbon dioxide in the atmosphere dissolves in the water and is absorbed by marine plants, and converted into organic matter. Other organisms eat the marine plants and form a carbon cycle, in much the same way as on land. Dead organisms sink to the bottom of the oceans and, over time, these carbon deposits form rock sediments.

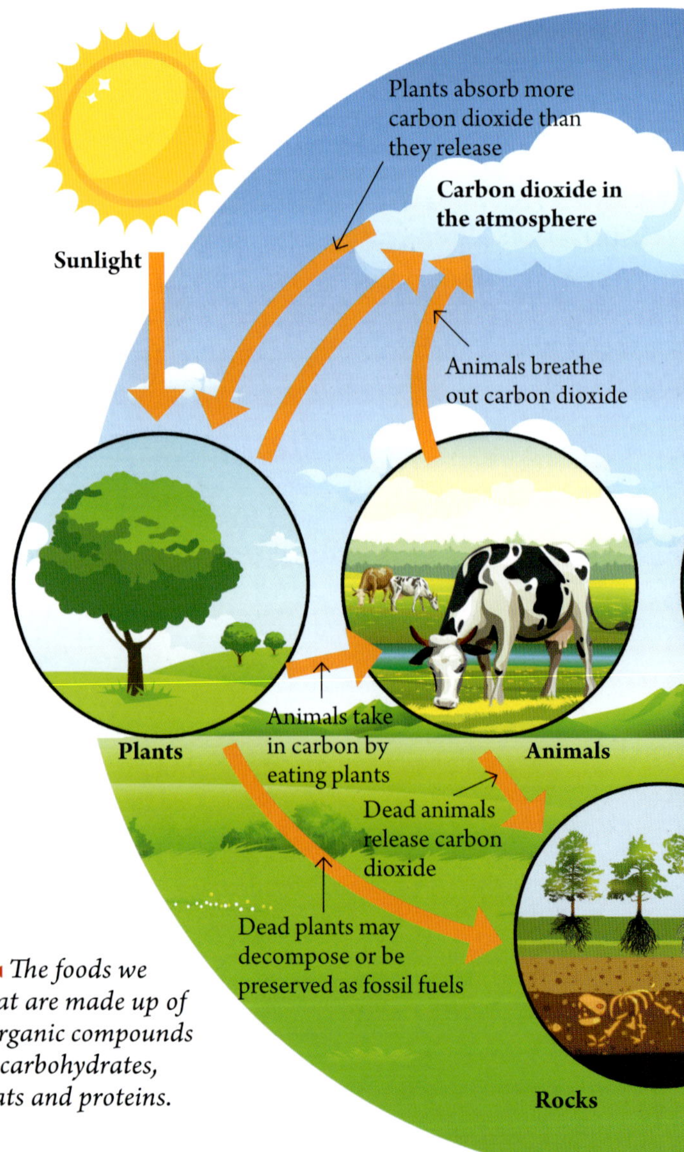

◄ *The foods we eat are made up of organic compounds - carbohydrates, fats and proteins.*

Essential Components of Life

All food components that are needed for our growth and development, such as carbohydrates, fats, proteins and vitamins, are organic compounds. In the human body, organic compounds like hormones and antibodies perform important functions to help us live healthy lives.

Polymers

Carbon atoms have the ability to form up to four chemical bonds with other atoms like hydrogen, oxygen and nitrogen. Molecules formed in this way can sometimes stretch to long chains with millions of repeated units. These giant molecules of repeating units are called polymers. Cellulose, which is a major component of plants, is a natural polymer. Plastics are artificial polymers that are made up of organic molecules. Polyethylene and polystyrene are examples of plastics that we use, and both are made of repeating units of carbon and hydrogen.

▲ Plastic materials are produced in large quantities to meet our daily demands.

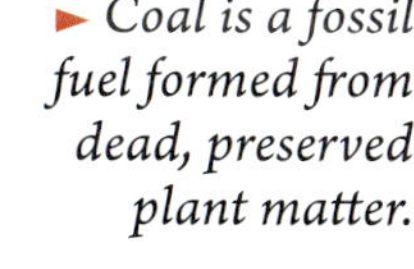

Oceans absorb carbon dioxide, but sea life also breathes it out

◄ *The carbon cycle is a continuous process that makes carbon available on Earth.*

Burning fossil fuels releases carbon dioxide

Humans dig up fossil fuels and burn them for energy

Carbon from ancient animals and plants forms fossil fuels

Fact File

On Earth, there are 10 times more organic compounds than inorganic compounds!

▲ *Naphthalene is a white, crystalline organic compound with a distinct odour.*

Organic Compounds

There are around 10 million organic compounds that we know about today and there may be even more that we haven't discovered yet! You can imagine how versatile and diverse they must be! Complex mixtures of organic compounds provide a variety of flavours, fragrances, and perfumes – some are pleasant, and others aren't so nice! For example, the chemicals in garlic and in a skunk's spray both contain organic compounds! The texture and properties of organic compounds vary greatly from one another.

► *Coal is a fossil fuel formed from dead, preserved plant matter.*

Fossil Fuels

Animals and plants that died millions of years ago get trapped under layers of earth, and transform into energy-rich fuels like coal, oil and natural gas. These fuels are organic compounds. Fossil fuels are used mainly for generating electricity and powering vehicles.

Materials

Materials are substances that we use for construction and manufacturing. Materials range from soft fabrics to hard metals. Each material serves a purpose based on its nature and properties. Scientists and engineers carefully choose the right materials to use for different purposes.

Early Materials

Thousands of years ago, our ancestors did not have access to the different kinds of materials we have now. They mostly depended on wood, stone, animal skin and hard parts of animals like bones, teeth and horns. Some materials, like skin and wood, were easier to mould and shape, but, when it came to making weapons or tools, stones were a better choice because they were hard and sharp. The earliest tools were made of basalt, sandstone, and flint, as well as different types of wood.

◄ *In ancient times, wood and stone were used together, to make tools and weapons.*

Materials Vary

Different materials have their own unique properties. Let's look at a few:

	Diamond	Granite
	Very Hard	Dense
	Diamond knives are used for cutting other hard materials	Building and construction purposes

	Clay
	Soft and Stretchable
	Making pots and ornamental vases

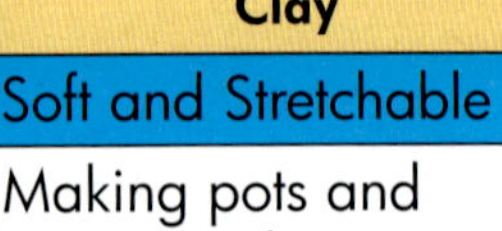

	Foam	Copper	Rubber
	Lightweight	Good conductor of electricity	Bad conductor of electricity
	Used in packing and shipping	Making electric wires and motors	Protective gloves and the outer insulator of electrical wires

▲ Nylon fibres are popular for their versatile uses and strength.

Synthetic Fibres

Synthetic fibres are manufactured by squeezing chemical mixtures through tiny holes. These fibres are light and flexible, and some are even waterproof! Nylon, rayon, acrylic and polyester are examples of synthetic fibres.

Plastics

The very first synthetic plastic was produced in 1907. Ever since, the production and use of different types of plastics has become common. Plastics have been used for everything from simple tableware to industrial grade pipes. The name 'plastic' is derived from the Greek word *plastikos* which means 'able to mould'. When heated, plastics can be moulded into almost any object!

Ceramics

Ceramics are made from a special kind of clay that hardens when it is baked at high temperatures. Ceramics, because they are bad conductors of electricity, are used as protective covering for power lines and spark plugs. Ceramics are easily breakable, which is why they are used carefully.

Composites

Composites are made by combining different substances to get the best features out of all the ingredients used. Concrete and fibreglass are examples of composites. Bulletproof clothing is made of a type of composite called Kevlar.

► Kevlar is used for making tough, bulletproof vests.

▲ Glass bottles and vases are shaped by blowing and shaping a hot, thick liquid.

Glass

Glass has been produced for thousands of years, and, for a long time, it was the only available transparent material. Glass is made by melting different minerals at a high temperature until they form a thick, sticky liquid that can be shaped by blowing. Glass is used for making windows, bottles and ornamental items.

The Earth's Resources

All materials, whether they are used for construction or fuel, come from the Earth. Some are natural resources like wood, stone, and metal. Others, like plastic and petrol, are produced after processing natural resources like fossil fuels or minerals.

Water

Fresh water is essential for life and is used for drinking and cooking. It is also necessary for growing crops and raising livestock. Even though 71% of the Earth is made up of water, only a very small percentage of this is fresh water. It is possible to convert sea water into fresh water, but this process consumes a lot of fuel and energy.

Land

Not all kinds of land are suitable for living on or cultivating food. Farmers look for tracts of land with fertile soil for growing food crops. Land is also needed for maintaining and raising livestock. Care must be taken to protect good, fertile soils by avoiding pollution and over-farming to get the most out of it.

▲ *Most of the freshwater on Earth is trapped in the form of large glaciers.*

◄ *Terrace farming is one of the common farming techniques practiced.*

Fossil Fuels

We extract coal, natural gas and oil from underneath the Earth's surface with the help of drills and mines. These fossil fuels power industries, homes and vehicles. Fossil fuels are limited resources. At the rate at which we're using them, they'll last for about another 80 - 120 years.

Fact File

Of the 3% of fresh water present on Earth, 2% is locked up in the form of glaciers and icecaps. This only leaves 1% in lakes, ponds and rivers that are available for our use.

▲ *The process of ocean drilling uses a mechanical bore to drill deep into the seabed in search of oil.*

Energy

Living on Earth, we all have many needs and so we use a lot of energy. The most common source of energy we use today comes from fossil fuels. When fossil fuels are burned, they also produce smoke and release harmful chemicals into the air. For the future, we will be looking at producing clean and efficient energy through non-polluting and more cost-effective means. Wind energy and solar energy are examples of clean sources of renewable energy.

▲ *Wood and timber in constant demand for many different purposes.*

Timber

In many parts of the world, forests are maintained for the purpose of growing trees that provide the wood needed for making paper, furniture, building materials and fuel. In sustainable forests, after trees are cut down, new ones are planted as replacements.

▲ *Windmills and solar panels are used for harvesting energy from wind and the Sun, respectively.*

What Force Does

Forces are like invisible powers. A force can be a push or a pull. We might not be able to see a force in action, but we can definitely observe its effects. Forces can do different things – they can change the shape of an object or hold things together.

Push and Pull forces

A force can act when two objects physically interact with or touch each other. Such a force is called a contact force. Think of a snooker cue hitting a ball on the table – the ball has been moved by a contact force.

Any force that can interact with an object, even from a distance, without the need for contact is called a field force. Gravity and magnetism are examples of field forces. An apple falling from a tree is pulled to the ground and a nail is drawn to a magnet without close contact because of field forces.

► *In order to make a football roll, it is kicked with force by the players.*

Let's look at a few different types of forces:

Nuclear force	Electromagnetic force	Gravity
Atoms are made up of electrons revolving around a nucleus. The strong force of attraction between the nucleus and the electrons in every atom is called nuclear force. In nuclear reactors, heavy atoms are split to release huge amounts of energy.	This force is exerted by charged particles in the presence of magnetic and electric fields. Electric doorbells and loudspeakers work based on electromagnetic forces.	Gravity is the force that is exerted on you and every other object on its surface. Gravity is the reason why we remain on the planet and don't drift away into space. Sometimes, in space, gravity can be extreme, as in the case of black holes, where everything close by is destructed.

▲ A suspension bridge involves a fine balancing act of gravity and upward tension.

The Balancing Act

Sometimes, forces act against each other and balance out. This can come in very useful for us. Can you guess how?

Let's look at how a suspension bridge works. We have already learnt that gravity attracts objects to the ground. In that case, how can a massive bridge stand without getting pulled down? The clue is in the steel cables that are holding it up. The upward tension exerted by the cables balance the gravity that acts on the bridge.

Two forces can also act together for an enhanced effect. For instance, when two people instead of one apply force and push a heavy object, the combined force makes it easier to accomplish the task.

Newton's Laws of Motion

First Law:
Everything remains at rest until a force acts on it.

Second Law:
A force can cause a push or pull that can increase an object's speed. The rate of change of speed depends on how big or small the force is.

Third Law:
For every force acting on an object, there is an equal and opposing force acting against it. You could say that forces work in pairs!

Friction

While walking on the floor, the reason that you don't slip is because there is friction between the floor and your feet. Friction is a kind of resistance produced as a result of one surface exerting a force on another. When two surfaces come into contact with each other, the atoms on the surfaces catch and snag each other. As a result, the surfaces rub or stick together and slow down slightly.

Air might look empty and light, but when you are cycling fast or running, you can sense the air pushing against you to slow you down. This is called drag. Drag is a type of friction, too. The faster you go, the harder you have to work against the drag.

► When a bicycle moves, the air pushes against the cyclist in a direction opposite to the movement.

Energy

Energy is the power inside everything. All organisms are 'living machines' that are powered by energy. Just like matter, energy can neither be created, nor destroyed. Energy can only be transformed from one form into another. All around the world, lots of energy is being used every single day. We use it all the time to run our businesses, fuel our transport, and power our homes.

About 80- 90% of the energy that we currently use comes from fossil fuels. When they are burned, the energy stored inside them is unlocked and used for different purposes.

▶ *In a gym, people expend energy to exercise and tone their muscles.*

Fact File

The energy from just one hour of sunlight is enough to power the entire world for one year!

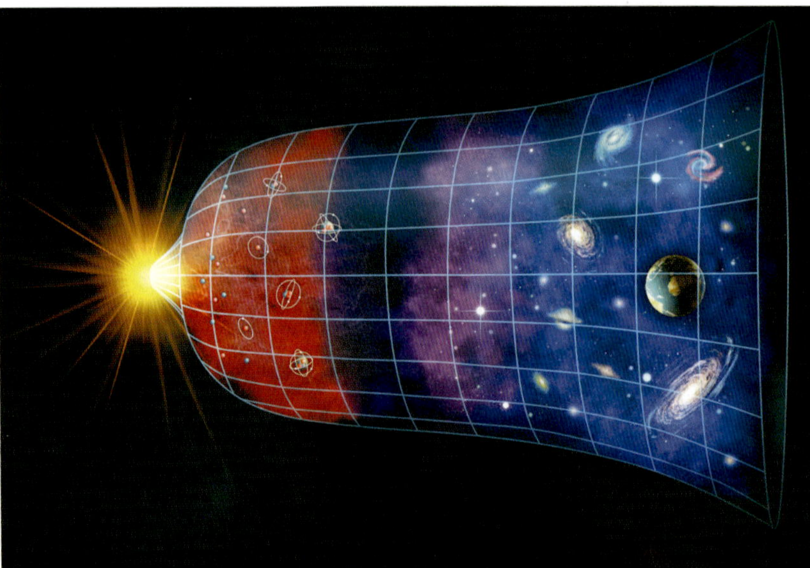

It All Started with a Big Bang!

The Universe came into existence around 14 billion years ago, after a massive explosion known as the Big Bang. The Universe was made entirely of pure energy, which later began to be converted into matter.

The Universe is full of energy of all kinds. Even things like a rock or a book have energy stored inside them. In fact, every object around you is either storing energy or using it up!

Types of Energy

1. Potential Energy: Any form of stored energy is called potential energy. For instance, when you push a ball up a hill, you have spent energy doing the work and the ball has gained potential energy. When you let go, the ball can use up this energy to roll back down!

◄ *When an arrow is fitted in a bow, it has stored potential energy.*

► *As the arrow is released, potential energy is converted into kinetic energy.*

2. Kinetic Energy: Things that are in motion possess kinetic energy. An example of kinetic energy is electricity. Electricity is produced by a flow of electrons inside something that can conduct electricity, such as a copper wire. When we say flow, we do not mean that the electrons are moving smoothly. Instead, atoms that acquire positive or negative charge have less or more electrons. As a result, they will either accept or donate electrons to become neutral. Imagine atoms exchanging electrons continuously! This creates a flow and thus generates a current of electricity.

3. Nuclear Energy: The energy stored up in the nucleus of an atom is called nuclear energy. Splitting certain atoms to release this energy is what powers nuclear power plants.

4. Chemical Energy: Energy that is released during chemical reactions is called chemical energy.

5. Sound Energy: Vibrating molecules produce sound by sending waves of energy into our ears.

6. Heat Energy: Atoms that make up matter vibrate constantly. When you apply heat, they vibrate faster. The hotter a substance is, the higher its heat energy levels. When one object is hotter than the other, heat will flow from the hotter object to the colder one. Take a cup of tea, for example. When you mix cold milk with piping hot tea, the tea becomes cooler because heat energy from the tea has been transferred to the milk.

▲ *Waves are powerful and the energy in the waves can be harnessed for use!*

7. Wave Energy: In seas and oceans, waves are formed when friction is created between the wind and the surface of the water. Did you know that waves can travel thousands of miles before reaching land? We can harness energy from waves by placing floating cylinders with electricity generators in the oceans.

▲ *Sound is produced by vibrating molecules.*

Light – Colour, Reflection and Refraction

Light is a form of energy. We can see things because of light. An interesting fact about light is that it can exist both as waves and as particles. Light is made up of particles called 'photons' which are tiny bundles of energy. The Sun is a major source of light. Light exhibits physical properties like reflection and refraction.

▶ *A table lamp converts electrical energy into light energy to help see and read in the dark.*

How We See Things

All objects emit light rays. We are able to see everything around us because light rays from objects enter our eyes through our pupils. Our eyes have lenses through which light passes and becomes focused. This focused light is transformed into an electric signal and is sent to the brain, which translates the image and reveals the colours, brightness, shapes, textures and other features of the objects we view. Light can pass through certain objects and not through others. Based on this property, we can classify objects into these three categories:

Opaque	Light rays cannot pass through the surface of opaque objects.
Translucent	Some light rays penetrate through the surface of translucent objects while some rays are reflected back.
Transparent	Almost all light rays pass through the surface of transparent objects, though some rays are reflected back (which is why we can still see them).

Light and Colours

Light is actually a mixture of lots of different colours. We know this because when you pass a beam of light through a prism (a triangular glass object), the light splits into the seven colours of the rainbow. Even though we say there are seven rainbow colours, there are actually an infinite number of colours in between that we are unable to see clearly!

▲ *White light splits into different colours when it passes through a prism.*

The Shadow Phenomenon

When light rays bounce against opaque objects that they are unable to pass through, they form a shadow corresponding to the shape and size of the object. The dark inner portion of a shadow is called the umbra while the slightly lighter outer edge is called penumbra. Next time you look at your shadow, see if you can identify these two regions!

Eclipses are formed by shadows of large objects like the Sun or Moon. A solar eclipse occurs when the Moon passes directly in front of the Sun and casts a shadow.

In ancient times people used shadows formed by the Sun to help them tell the time! A sundial has markings to denote every hour of daylight and a projecting piece called a 'gnomon'. As the Sun moves across the sky, the shadows cast by the 'gnomon' change too. The position of the shadow is helpful for telling the time!

A shadow can be long or short depending on what time of the day it is!

Reflection and Refraction

When light rays strike a surface and bounces back, it is called reflection. Most surfaces absorb light, but mirrors reflect all the light rays that strike their surfaces. You can see yourself in a mirror because of its reflective property.

Mirrors are flat surfaces made of glass with a shiny metal like silver coated on one side. Since glass has a very smooth surface, the light rays that strike it do not get scattered in random directions, but instead, reflect and meet at a point. This process is called convergence.

Other smooth surfaces like a still pond or polished floor can also exhibit reflective properties.

Fun mirrors are convex (bulged inwards) or concave (bulged outwards) to provide all kinds of funny distortions! While flat mirrors reflect the light straight back from the source, the convex and concave mirrors alter the way light is reflected into our eyes.

Refraction is a phenomenon by which light rays bend when passing from one medium to another, for instance, from air to water.

Put a pencil in a glass of water and you'll notice that it looks bent. This is because of refraction.

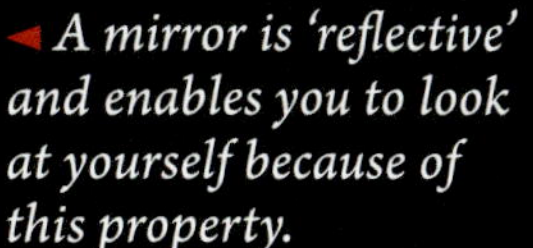

A mirror is 'reflective' and enables you to look at yourself because of this property.

Light – Lasers, Microscopes and Telescopes

Lasers, microscopes and telescopes are examples of optical devices. 'Optical' means 'related to light'. All of these devices use light in some form. In a laser, light is amplified inside special tubes. In the case of microscopes and telescopes, light is focused on lenses to magnify objects that are otherwise impossible to see.

Laser Technology

A laser is an instrument that produces a very powerful beam of light. The word 'laser' stands for 'Light Amplification by Stimulated Emission of Radiation' – this definition also explains how a laser works:

A laser consists of a specially-designed tube with mirrors at both ends. This tube is filled with a material like gas, crystal or liquid. A powerful lamp (or something similar) adds energy to the material. The electrons inside each atom absorb this energy and move from one energy level to another. Eventually, when they return to their original level, the electrons emit 'photons', which are particles of light. All the released photons have the same wavelength and form a powerful, concentrated beam.

Lasers have many uses. Most commonly, they are used in colourful light displays, holograms and in CD/DVD players.

► *Ranging from entertainment to surgery, lasers have many uses.*

▲ *Colourful laser light displays involve many powerful laser beams for entertainment.*

Magnifying the World

Microscopes work like magnifying glasses, but they can magnify objects even more. This is because a light microscope usually has two lenses and the combined effect provides higher magnification.

Anton van Leeuwenhoek was one of the first people to experiment with different types of lenses to come up with a magnifying device to view tiny organisms. Since then, advanced microscopes have been developed. The working mechanism of a light microscope is simple: the object to be viewed is kept on a glass slide and mounted on the microscope. A mirror focusing natural light or an in-built lamp in the microscope illuminates the slide. The light rays pass through the slide and then through the magnifying lenses, before striking the eyes. With the help of microscopes we can see minuscule cells, tiny microbes and many other things that are not visible to the naked eye.

▲ *A microscope focuses light on tiny objects to magnify them and show small details.*

Telescopes for Understanding Space

Optical telescopes work in a very similar way to microscopes. Since our eyes have limitations, a telescope serves to extend our sense of sight. Binoculars are a pair of identical telescopes mounted side by side. In fact, in the early days, they were called binocular telescopes. A good pair of binoculars can reveal as many details as an amateur telescope and are great for activities such as bird-watching.

A telescope uses glass lenses to capture light rays from distant planets, galaxies, stars and other objects that are very far away.

The Large Binocular Telescope is located in Arizona. It is one of the largest and most powerful optical telescopes on Earth.

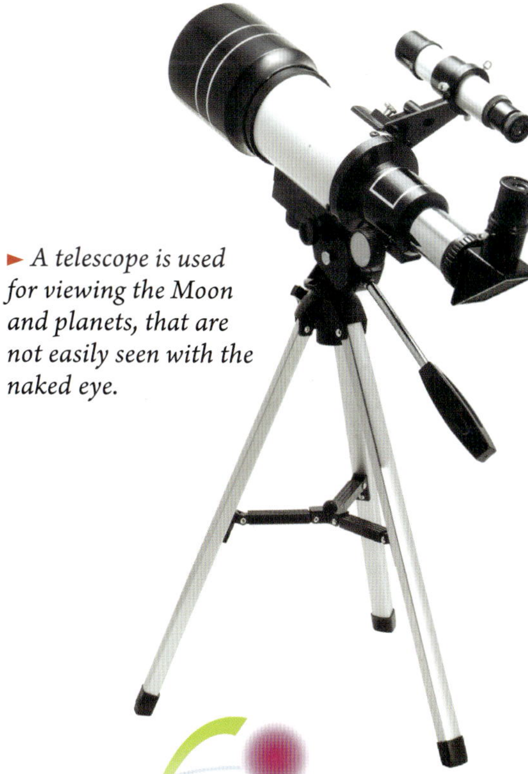

▶ *A telescope is used for viewing the Moon and planets, that are not easily seen with the naked eye.*

▲ *The Large Binocular Telescope is located on top of Mount Graham, at a height of 10,700 feet.*

Fact File

Doctors use lasers instead of scalpels during surgery to make precise cuts. The advantage of using lasers is that they are more accurate, and cuts can be closed without using stitches.

Electricity – Current and Magnetism

Electricity is powered by electrons, the negatively charged particles that revolve around the nucleus of an atom. Electricity powers many things that we use every day, as well as extremely large industries and powerful trains. From the humble light bulb to the thrilling roller-coaster, we need electricity for running everything!

How is Electricity Produced?

There are two kinds of electricity – static and current. Static electricity is produced when electrons gather together in one place, while current electricity is the result of a flow of electrons.

Rub a balloon against your sweater and it will become negatively charged as electrons move and accumulate there. When you bring the balloon close to your hair, a few more negatively charged electrons from your hair will move to the balloon. After losing the electrons, your hair should acquire a slight positive charge and stick to the balloon for a few seconds.

Current electricity powers everything from small domestic appliances to large factories! An electric current is actually a flow of electrons, caused by millions of atoms exchanging electrons continuously.

▲ *Power lines carry electricity from the source of generation to houses and industries.*

Electric circuit

An electric circuit is a complete path through which electricity flows from the source, all the way to the object that is to be powered. Not all materials can be used for making circuits. Some materials are good conductors of electricity while others are not.

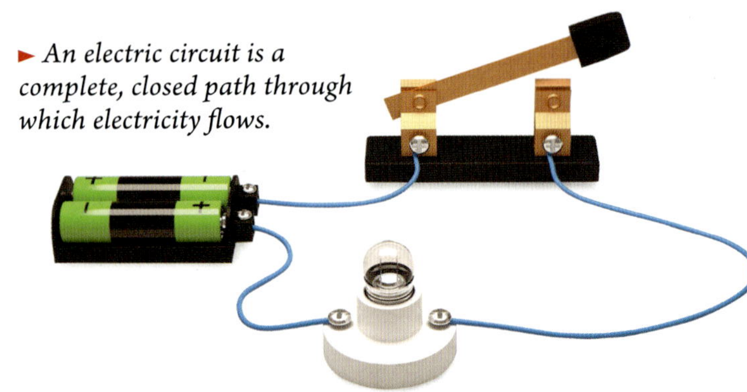

► *An electric circuit is a complete, closed path through which electricity flows.*

Conductors versus Insulators

Do you know why copper is used in electric wires? It is because copper is an excellent conductor of electricity. It allows the flow of electrons that produces electricity. On the other hand, other materials like plastic, wood, or rubber, stop electricity from passing through. Bad conductors of electricity are known as insulators. In order to make electric wires safe, copper wires are surrounded by an outer layer made of an insulating material like plastic so that we don't get an electric shock when we touch them.

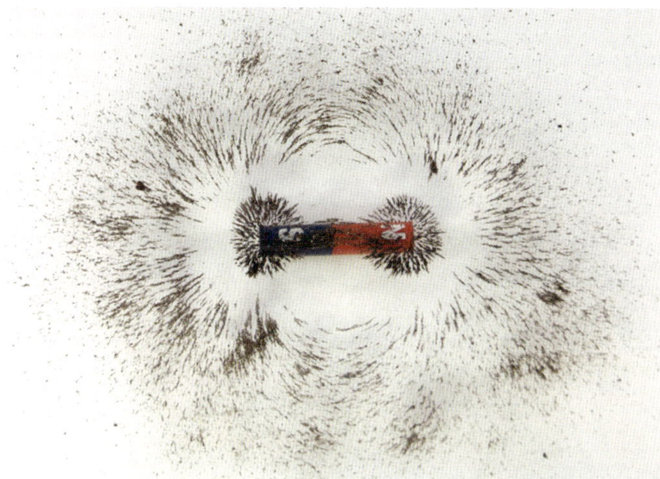

▲ *In the presence of a bar magnet, iron filings are attracted to the poles and display a magnetic field of attraction around it.*

What is electromagnetism?

Electricity and magnetism are produced as a result of electrons and how they move. Electromagnetism is the process by which a flow of electric current can create a magnetic field.

If an iron nail is taken and wound tightly around a coil of wire and if electricity is passed through this wire, the nail will temporarily become an electromagnet. That is, it behaves like a magnet as long as electricity is passed through it. This electromagnet will be able to attract other nails and magnetic substances. It will also have a north and a south pole like an actual magnet.

▲ *Electric wires are commonly made of copper and are surrounded by a layer of plastic for safety.*

Magnetism

Magnetism is also the result of the movement of electrons. While electricity involves the flow of electrons, magnetism is produced by the spin of electrons. This spinning motion creates an electric current and each electron acts like a tiny magnet.

Why are some substances magnetic while others are not? In order to answer this question, let's look at two examples, iron and paper. Iron is a strongly magnetic substance while paper isn't magnetic at all. In iron, almost all electrons within the atoms spin in the same direction and the collective effect results in magnetism. In paper, there are nearly equal numbers of electrons that spin in opposite directions, thus cancelling each other out.

Fact File

Electricity can flow only in a closed circuit or path. Switching an appliance on, closes the circuit and allows the electricity to flow in and power the device.

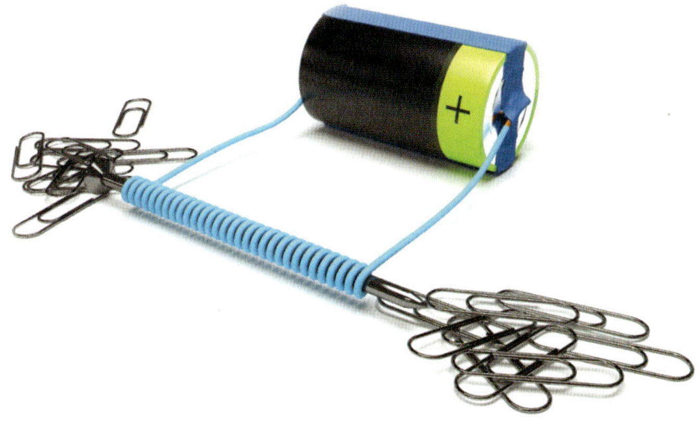

◄ *This electromagnet has a nail wound tightly with coils of wire to transform it into a magnet in the presence of electricity.*

DNA, Genes, Evolution and Life Forms

All living organisms that are similar, are classified into one of the different groups based on their physical and biological features. Organisms that are identical and capable of producing offspring together are called 'species'.

These are a few major groups of different living organisms:

Bacteria

Microscopic single-celled organisms. They come in different shapes and sizes and usually depend on other organisms (hosts) for survival. Some bacteria are useful while others can cause diseases and harm us. Lactobacilli that help make yogurt is a useful microbe, while Clostridium species cause food poisoning.

Fungi	Algae	Plants	Animals
Lives mostly on dead and decaying matter. Fungi absorb nutrients from living or dead matter directly into the cells. Mushrooms and mould are examples of fungi. Mushrooms grow and feed on dead logs or leaf litter and absorb moisture from the wood and soil.	This is a group of organisms that use sunlight just like plants to make their own food. Green algae scum in lakes and Seaweeds are examples. Unlike plants, algae don't have leaves, roots or stems and don't reproduce through seeds.	Plants are capable of harvesting sunlight through a process called photosynthesis. There are two types of plants: flowering plants such as oak, apple, cherry blossom and non-flowering plants like pine, spruce and fir.	Animals depend on plants as a major source of food and energy. There are many types of animals ranging from the jellyfish to apes. Among the advanced animals, the presence or absence of a backbone classifies them into vertebrates and invertebrates respectively.

Genes, DNA and Chromosomes

A gene is a section of DNA that carries the information for manufacturing a specific protein. This protein could play an important role in any of the different vital functions, like regulating blood sugar and many other important functions. Our genes determine how we look and how we function.

In many organisms, DNA is organised into separate lengths called chromosomes. Chromosomes consist of proteins that coil DNA and pack them tightly. Chromosomes occur in pairs and are found inside the cell's nucleus. Chromosomes are usually shaped like the letter 'X'.

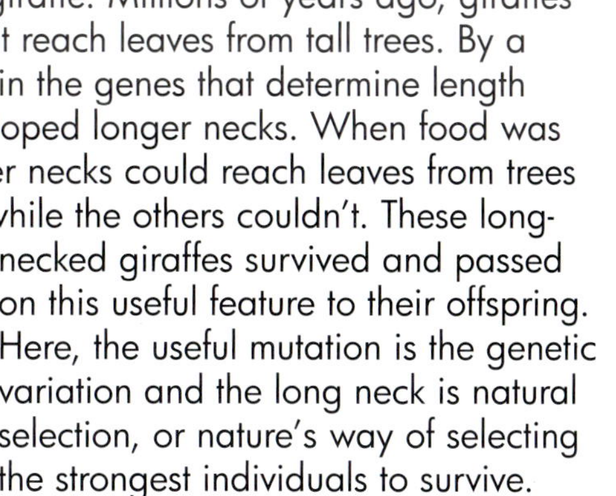

▲ *DNA strands are compacted into chromosomes and are present inside the nucleus of a cell.*

DNA and Genes

All the instructions necessary for a single cell to develop into a full-sized organism is coded in the genetic material or DNA. DNA stands for deoxyribonucleic acid. Parents pass on their DNA to their offspring, which is why children resemble their parents. The process by which DNA makes identical copies is called replication.

Evolution

Evolution is a continual process of change of an organism over many generations through natural selection and genetic variation. Let's take the example of a giraffe. Millions of years ago, giraffes had short necks and couldn't reach leaves from tall trees. By a chance mutation or change in the genes that determine length of neck, a few giraffes developed longer necks. When food was scarce, the giraffes with taller necks could reach leaves from trees while the others couldn't. These long-necked giraffes survived and passed on this useful feature to their offspring. Here, the useful mutation is the genetic variation and the long neck is natural selection, or nature's way of selecting the strongest individuals to survive.

Charles Darwin was a biologist who played an important role in establishing the theory of modern evolution and published it in his work entitled 'Origin of Species'.

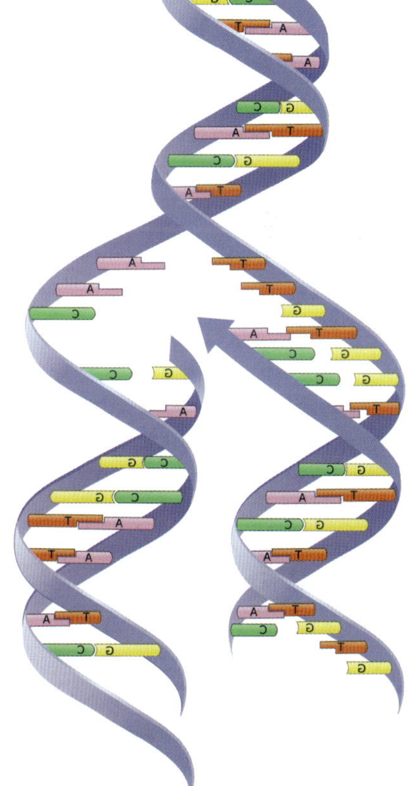

▲ *Through a process called replication, DNA strands separate and form exact copies.*

Fact File

If you could unravel the entire DNA from all the cells in your body and lay it end to end, it would stretch from the Earth to the Sun hundreds of times.

Plants, Photosynthesis, Habitats and Ecosystems

Plants are a group of organisms capable of manufacturing their own food with the help of sunlight and water. This mechanism is called photosynthesis. 'Photo' means 'Light' and 'synthesis' means 'making'. The energy from the Sun is harvested for making sugars and helps plants live, develop and reproduce. Plants form the basis of all land-based habitats on Earth.

How Photosynthesis Happens

Plants are adapted to synthesize (manufacture) their own food in the form of simple sugars, with the help of sunlight, water (H_2O) and carbon dioxide (CO_2). Oxygen (O_2) is released in the process.

Stomata are tiny openings present in the leaves of plants through which carbon dioxide is taken in. Water is absorbed through the roots and passes through the stem to reach the leaves. Most leaves are green in colour because of a pigment called chlorophyll present inside cell organelles called 'chloroplasts'. Chlorophyll and other pigments are important for photosynthesis. Sugars produced here are mostly used up for growth and development, while some are stored in roots, fruits or leaves. When leaves age and stop producing pigments, they turn brown and fall off the tree/plant.

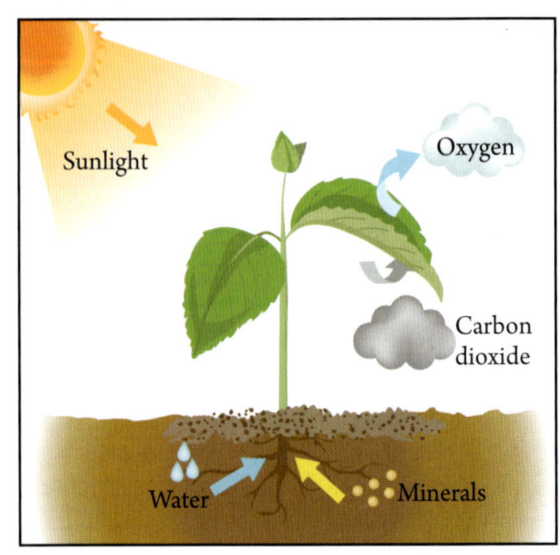

▲ An Arctic fox's home is the Tundra while lions are found in the Savannah grasslands.

Habitats

A habitat refers to a place that is suitable for the survival and existence of a species. For the Arctic fox, a snowy mountain is an ideal habitat while Savannah grasslands provide the right environment for a lion.

All the plants and animals living in a particular habitat are collectively referred to as a community. In a community, the different members interact with each other; some are prey and some are predators, while others are mutually beneficial to each other.

Some of the major habitats on Earth are:

1. **Savannah Grassland**
2. **Polar Ice Region**
3. **Tropical Rain forest**
4. **Desert**
5. **Tundra**

6. **Mediterranean region**
7. **Temperate grasslands**
8. **Deciduous forest**
9. **Coniferous forest**
10. **Mountain**

▲ Habitats (Clockwise): Tropical rainforest; Desert; Tundra; Mountain

Ecosystems

An ecosystem is a network of different plants and animals that live together and interact in a particular habitat. All the members of an ecosystem depend on each other for their existence. Let us look at an example: In grasslands, the lions depend on deer for food and survival. The deer in turn depend on the grass, plants and shrubs. How can lions benefit deer? Like with any other species, the right balance of population is needed. If there were no lions, the deer population would increase exponentially and cause intense competition for food and living space.

A food chain ends with predators and starts with plants. Many interlinked food chains form a food web.

▲ A food web shows the different predators and preys in a particular habitat.

Inventions and Discoveries

Many significant inventions and discoveries, whether technological, scientific or historical, have changed how we view and treat our planet and how we function within our cultures and societies. The following timeline presents some of the most important inventions, from 15,000 BC to the present day.

2 – 3.3 million years
STONE TOOLS They were used by the early man for a variety of purposes, the main use probably being to fend off attacks from wild animals.

3000 BC
BRONZE TOOLS Ancient people began to melt and use alloys like bronze to craft weapons and tools that were more effective than those made of stone.

2400 BC
ABACUS This simple device was used for counting and is thought to have been invented in Babylonia.

15,000 BC - - - - - - - - - - - 7500 BC - - - - - - - - - - - - 5000 BC - - - - - - - - - - - 2500 BC - - - -

---

3000 BC
COTTON CLOTHING
The first cotton clothing is believed to have been made around 5,000 years ago in the Indus Valley.

20,000 BC
POTTERY The art of crafting and baking clay into pots and vessels enabled the storing of food and water.

300 BC
LIGHTHOUSE The earliest lighthouse is considered to have been in Pharos, Egypt. The light from the fire in the lighthouse, was supposedly visible for at least 20 miles.

105 BC
PAPER It was first made in China by the inventor, Cai Lun. Paper paved the way for mass printing of books, which enabled the sharing of ideas among many people.

600 CE
WINDMILL The first documented windmill is thought to have been built in Persia. The wind power was used for grinding grain and pumping water.

700 CE
ZERO It is believed that zero was treated as a number first in India in the 7th century.

1430s
PRINTING PRESS Even though the printing press existed in China before this date, before Gutenberg's invention of the printing press, books were copied by hand in Europe.

1608
TELESCOPE A Dutch spectacle-maker, Hans Lippershey, invented the first telescope. Galileo Galilee improved the design and used the telescope for viewing distant planets.

-------------- 100 CE -------------------- 1500 ---------------------- 1600 -------------------------- 1700 -----------------

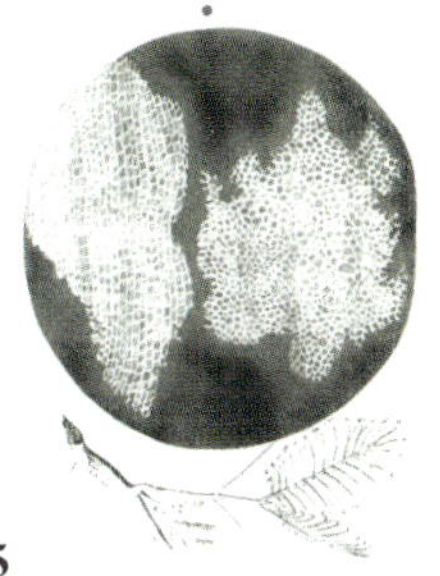

1665
CELL Robert Hooke viewed a slice of cork under a microscope and discovered that it was made up of individual units which he called 'cells'. A cell is considered the basic unit of living organisms.

1100s
MARINER'S COMPASS The mariner's compass consisted of a magnet that always pointed towards the Earth's geographical north. It was used by Chinese sailors to navigate their ships.

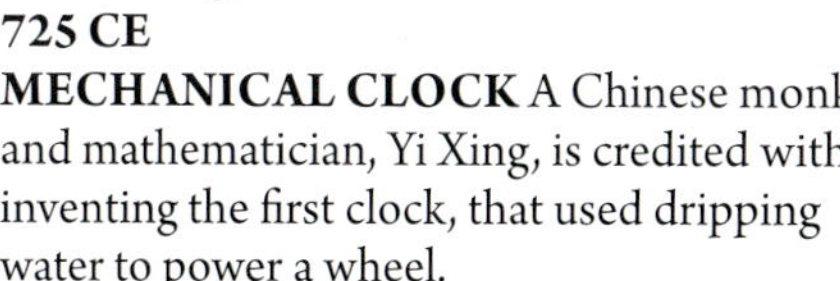

725 CE
MECHANICAL CLOCK A Chinese monk and mathematician, Yi Xing, is credited with inventing the first clock, that used dripping water to power a wheel.

1712
STEAM ENGINE Thomas Newcomen was the first person to use steam for powering a water-pumping engine. Steam has since been used for powering trains, boats and cars.

1876

TELEPHONE Alexander Graham Bell invented the most practical model of telephone. The telephone played a very important role in long distance communication until it was replaced by cellular phones.

1796

SMALLPOX VACCINE Edward Jenner invented the smallpox vaccine when he showed that injecting a substance from a cowpox lesion could protect against smallpox.

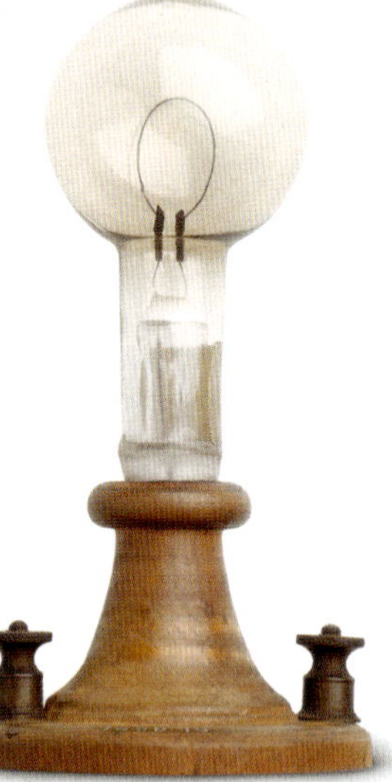

1878

LIGHT BULB Edison's electric light bulb began a revolution of lighting up the world. Until the invention of light bulb, people mostly depended on candles and gas flames.

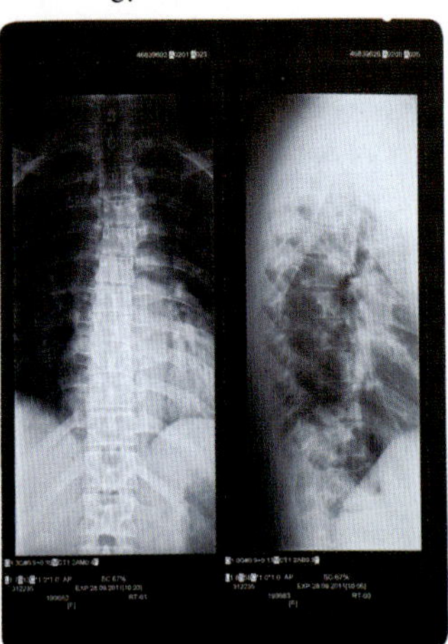

1951 – 53

DNA DOUBLE HELIX Watson and Crick described the structure of DNA as a double helix with the help of an image of DNA taken by Rosalind Franklin with an X-ray Crystallography device.

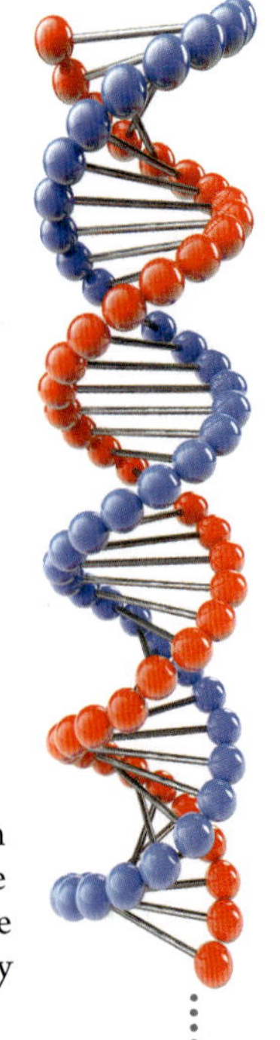

1800 — **1900** — **1950**

1856 - 1863

GENETICS AND INHERITANCE An Austrian monk, Gregor Mendel, did detailed studies on pea plants and put forward important genetic theories on inheritance.

1829

BRAILLE ALPHABETS Louis Braille, who lost his sight at an early age, came up with the idea of a raised dots alphabet system, which would enable blind people to read.

1926

TELEVISION John Logie Baird invented a way of transmitting pictures through radio waves.

1928

PENICILLIN

The first antibiotic, penicillin, was discovered by Alexander Fleming after observing how a fungal mould, Penicillium, stopped certain bacteria from growing around it.

1903

WINGED AIRCRAFT The brothers, Wilbur and Oliver Wright created an engine-powered glider that was one of the important steps towards the invention of modern-day aeroplanes.

1969

MOON LANDING It was a milestone moment when Neil Armstrong and Buzz Aldrin first landed on the Moon, marking a new achievement in the field of space research.

1973

CELLULAR PHONE Even though the telephone had been invented decades before, cell phones that could be carried around were developed in 1973. Martin Cooper of Motorola Corporation invented the first cellular phone.

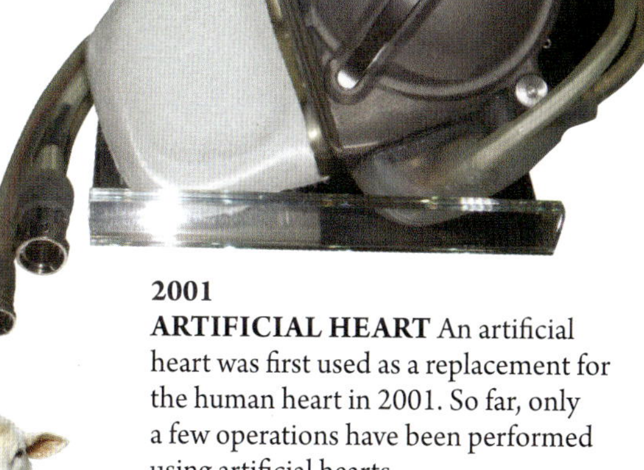

2001

ARTIFICIAL HEART An artificial heart was first used as a replacement for the human heart in 2001. So far, only a few operations have been performed using artificial hearts.

1996

CLONING OF DOLLY The power of genetic engineering became evident after the first successful cloning of a sheep called Dolly. Cloning involves making an exact copy of genetic material.

1975 ---- **2000** ---- **2010**

1974

INTERNET The first internet service provider was created. The internet is a revolutionary technology enabling the sharing of information from any part of the world to another, quickly and easily.

1994

SMARTPHONE Smartphones combine features of a computer and a phone in a compact, touchscreen-based device. Simon, the first smartphone, had apps, internet access and a touchscreen operated with stylus.

2012

DRIVERLESS CAR The testing of self-driving cars began in 2012. These cars are expected to create the next revolution in transportation.

1977

PERSONAL COMPUTERS Early computers were large and expensive. Affordable and compact PCs were first introduced in 1977.

A First Introduction to Science

ENCYCLOPEDIA of LEARNING

DISCOVER
LIGHT
SOUND & MOTION

WAVES

In simple terms, a wave is any disturbance or vibration that transfers from one point to another, transferring energy but not matter. Waves are everywhere around us. We might not be able to see or recognize them, but they play a vital role in our day-to-day lives.

Medium for Waves

Waves can be mechanical or electromagnetic. Not all waves require a medium to travel through. A medium is any substance that transmits waves. The medium consists of interacting particles. The particles that make up a medium vibrate when waves pass through and are temporarily displaced from their original position. The interacting particles of the medium enable the waves to travel from one place to another.

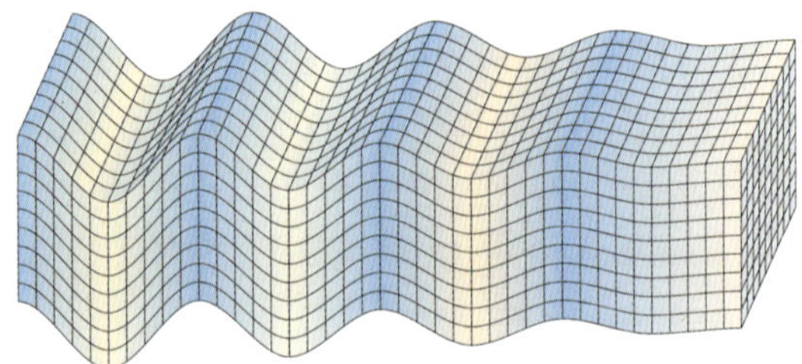
⦿ *Waves vibrate particles in a medium as they pass through.*

The ripples in a pond travel through the medium, water. Sound waves travel through air, liquids and solids. Sound waves cannot be transferred in vacuum or empty space. Light waves, being electromagnetic waves, can travel in vacuum. Seismic waves, originating from under the Earth's surface are mechanical waves that, like sound, require a medium for transmission.

⦿ *A technician adjusts various aspects of sound waves for best results.*

Wave Properties

Waves have certain properties such as amplitude, frequency, period, speed and wavelength. A wave is represented in a graph with the highest point called a crest and the lowest point called a trough.

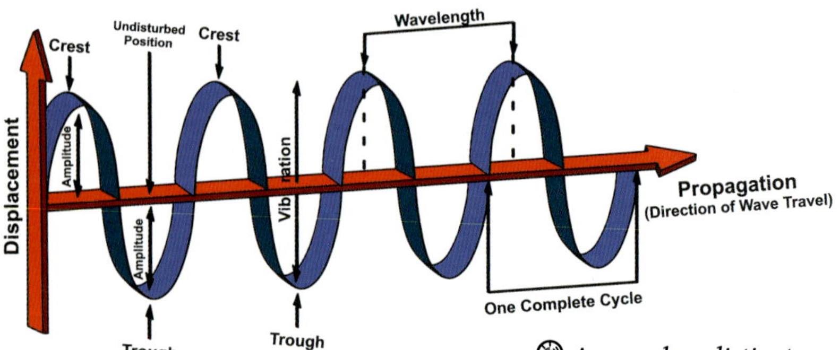

⦿ *A wave has distinct high and low points called crests and troughs respectively*

Amplitude: The maximum displacement of a wave from its rest position is called amplitude. It is calculated by measuring the height of the wave from rest position. Amplitude measures the intensity or strength of a wave. A sound wave with higher amplitude will be louder than another with lower amplitude.

Wavelength: The distance between two crests or two troughs on a wave is called the wavelength.

Frequency: The number of times a wave cycles per second is called the frequency. By knowing the wavelength and frequency, the velocity (rate of change of speed) of a wave can be calculated using the formula: Velocity = Wavelength x Frequency

Types of Waves

Waves are of two basic types: mechanical and electromagnetic.

Mechanical waves require a medium to travel. The wave travels by vibration and transfer of energy from one particle to another. Sound is a type of mechanical wave. It can travel through solids, liquids and air, but it cannot transmit across vacuum (empty space). Electromagnetic waves do not require a medium and instead travel through electrical and magnetic fields generated by charged particles. Light and X-rays are examples of electromagnetic radiation.

Ripples forming on water is an example of mechanical waves.

Light is an electromagnetic wave that can travel through vacuum.

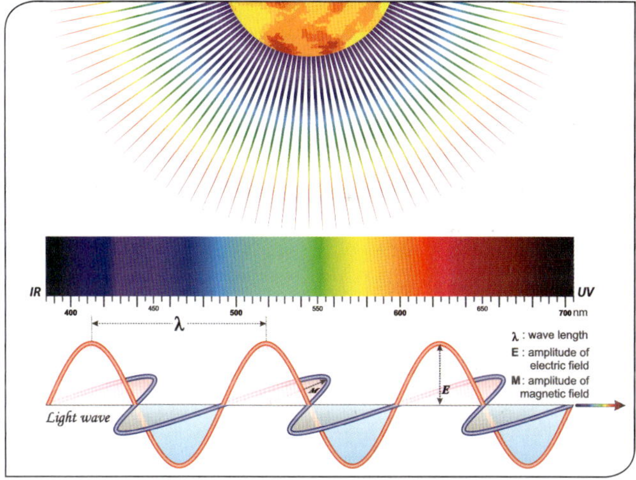

Longitudinal and Transverse Waves

A longitudinal wave generates vibrations or disturbances in parallel with the wave. A transverse wave generates vibrations or disturbances that move perpendicular to the wave.

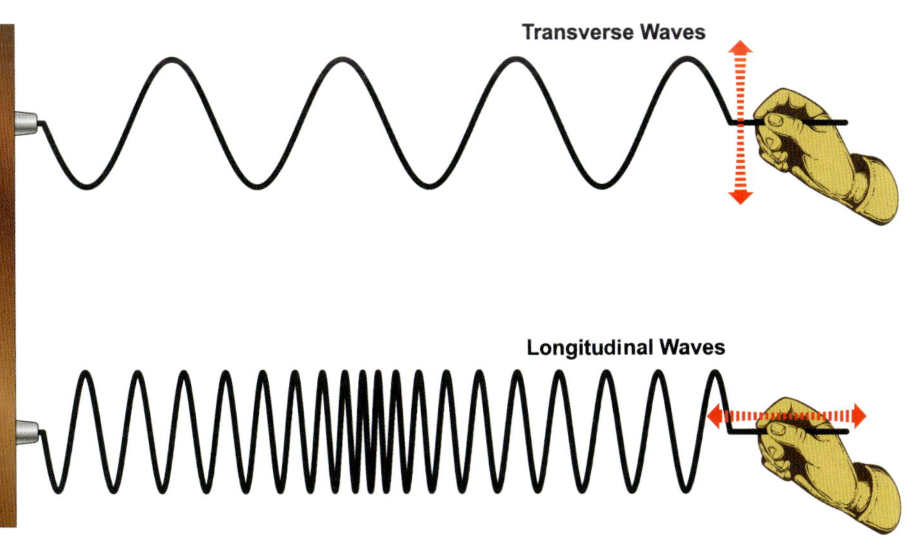

Waves usually propagate in two forms - transverse or longitudinal.

LIGHT

Light is everywhere around us. Life on Earth is not possible without light. We perceive light in the form of thousands of colours, though it exists in forms that are invisible to the human eye. Light is a kind of energy that travels in the form of vibrating waves of electricity and magnetism. Sun is the main source of light in the solar system. The study of light is known as optics.

When white light passes through a prism, it splits into different colours.

We perceive light in different forms and colours.

What Produces Light?

Light is produced when atoms get 'excited'. Atoms are the fundamental components that make up all matter in the universe. An atom has a nucleus in the centre, with protons and neutrons, carrying a positive charge. Negatively charged electrons revolve around the nucleus at specific distances.

When the electrons remain in their stable position or ground state, they do not absorb or emit energy. However, when an electron is moved from its stable position to higher energy levels, the electron gains energy and the atom is said to be 'excited'. The electron prefers to return to stability or to its lower energy level. To achieve this, the electron loses the energy in the form of a 'photon', which is a packet of light. A photon is an elementary particle without mass or electric charge and moves at the speed of 3×10^8 metres per second. We can see light as photons which fall on our eyes and are detected by receptors in the eye and brain.

Christiaan Huygens, a Dutch scientist, proposed that light is made up of waves.

Dual Nature of Light

For several decades, scientists pondered and argued about the nature of light. In the 17th century, the renowned physicist, Isaac Newton, became one of the first to study light in detail. He proposed that light was a stream of particles or 'corpuscles' that could strike objects. A Dutch scientist and Newton's contemporary, Christiaan Huygens argued that light was not made up of particles, but waves.

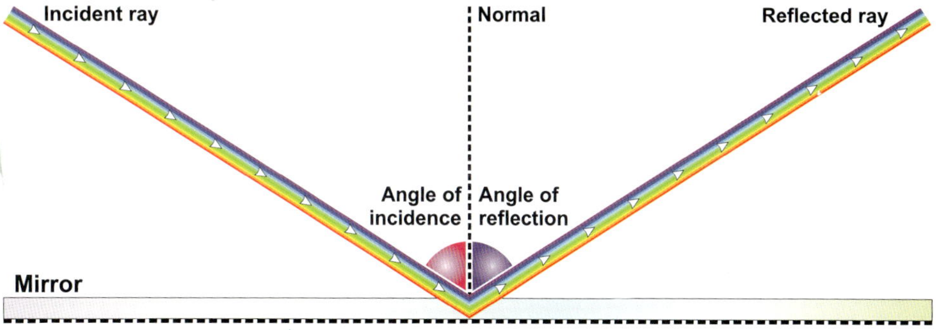

Reflection

Reflection from a mirror

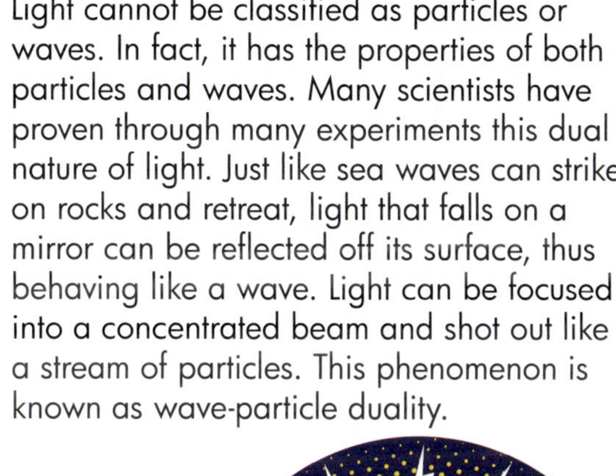

Light can be reflected off a surface indicating its wave nature

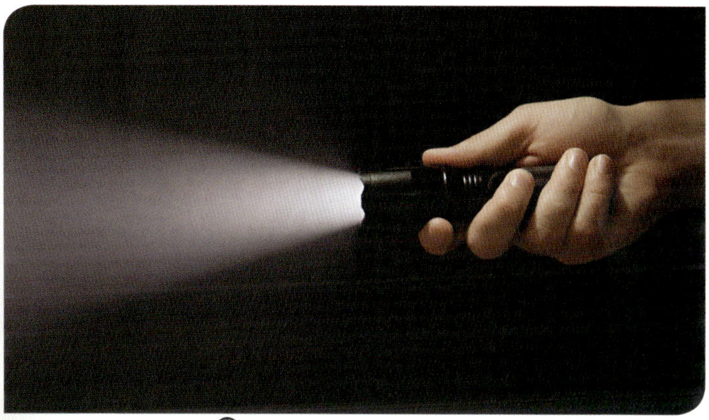

Light behaves like particles because it can be focused into a concentrated beam.

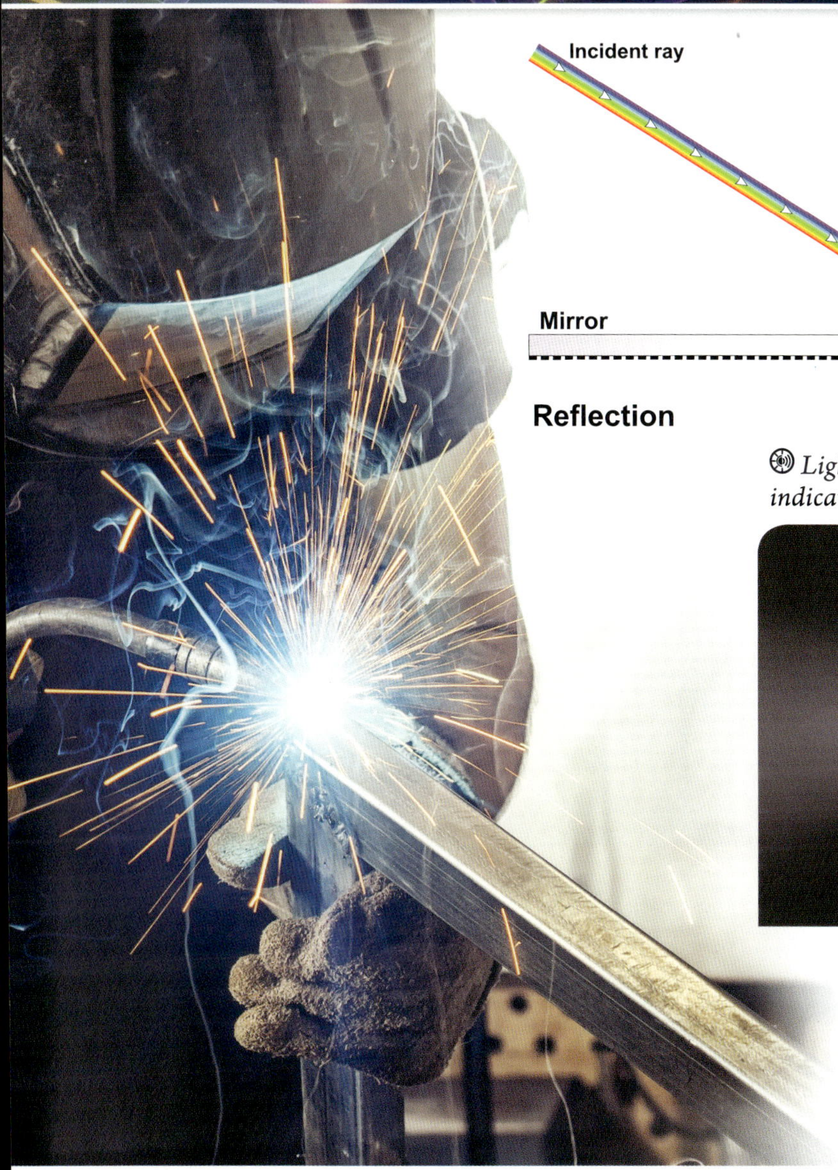

Light cannot be classified as particles or waves. In fact, it has the properties of both particles and waves. Many scientists have proven through many experiments this dual nature of light. Just like sea waves can strike on rocks and retreat, light that falls on a mirror can be reflected off its surface, thus behaving like a wave. Light can be focused into a concentrated beam and shot out like a stream of particles. This phenomenon is known as wave-particle duality.

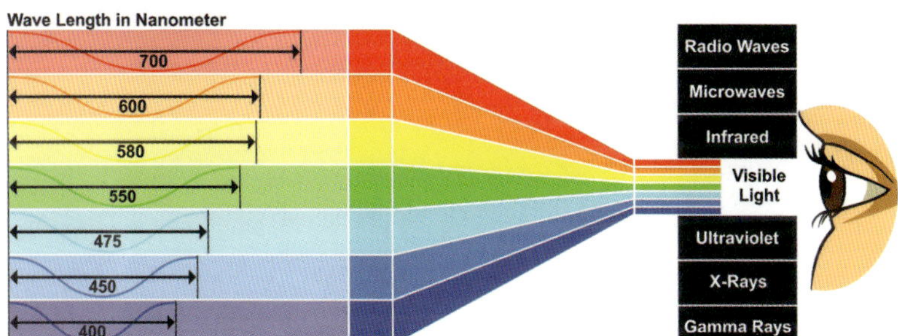

The visible spectrum is the only portion of electromagnetic radiation that we can perceive.

Visible Light Spectrum

Even though light exists in different wavelengths and energies, humans can perceive only a small portion of it, namely the visible spectrum in the 400 – 700 nanometres range. When light passes through a glass prism, it splits into different colours: red, orange, yellow, green, blue, indigo and violet. Thomas Young became the first scientist to measure the wavelengths of the different colours of the visible spectrum.

We perceive the universe from what our eyes can visualize. The light from the stars we see has travelled across millions of miles. Today, we have advanced telescopes that can perceive the universe in much better detail. Light has been manipulated and applied in technologies such as lasers, holography and fibre optic based communication.

Fact File

Humans can only perceive visible light. Bees can detect ultraviolet rays while rattlesnakes can see infrared radiation.

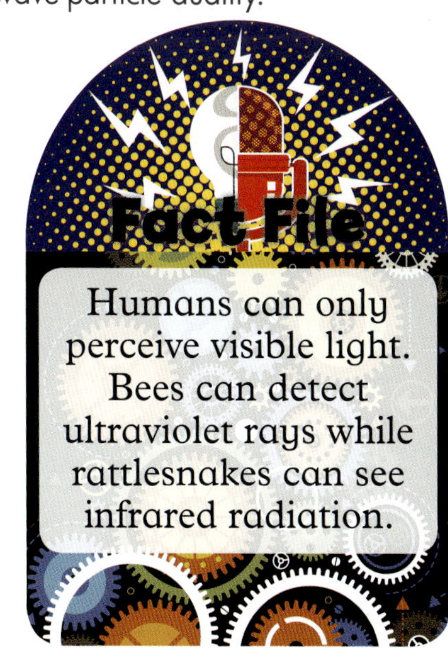

PROPERTIES OF LIGHT

Since light is a form of wave, it exhibits certain properties specific to waves. Light exhibits certain characteristic features, that can be observed from natural sources (such as sunlight) or artificial sources (such as lamps). The best known properties of light are reflection, refraction, diffraction and interference.

Light, as waves, exhibits different properties.

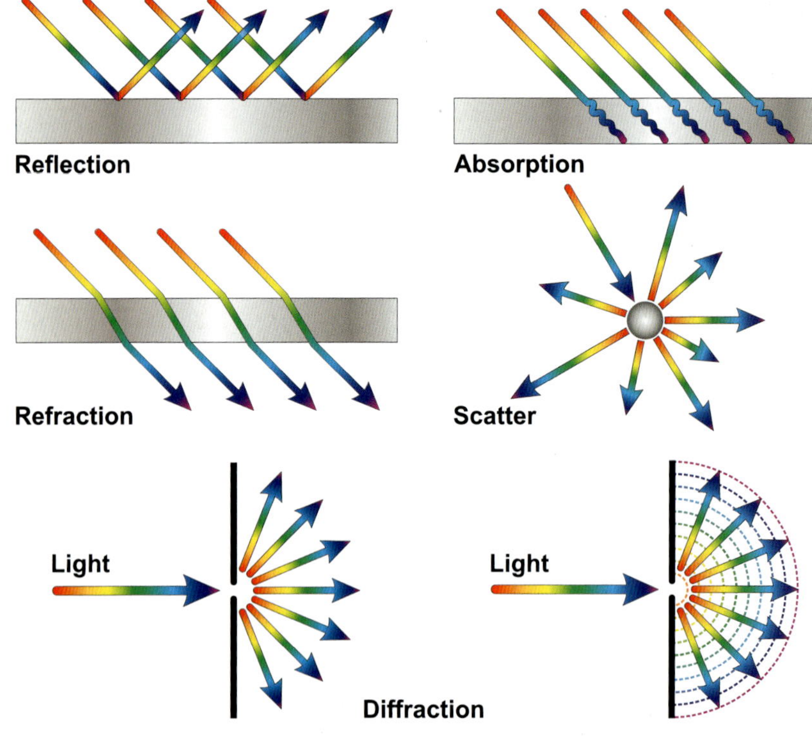

Reflection

Light has the ability to reflect off things. The reason why we are able to perceive light is because of its ability to reflect off objects into our eyes. When a narrow beam of light is shone onto a polished surface, it bounces back as a narrow beam. This type of reflection is called specular reflection. A mirror is an example of a highly polished surface. When light bounces off rough objects, it scatters all over the place and this is known as diffuse reflection. This is the reason why we cannot see our reflection on rough surfaces such as wood or paper.

A mirror is a polished surface that reflects light falling on it.

Refraction

When it travels through vacuum (empty space), light travels in a straight line. When it travels through different mediums such as air or water, light bends depending on the density of the medium. The denser a material is, the more dramatically light bends when it passes through it. This phenomenon is known as refraction. Refraction happens at the junction where one medium meets another.

The reason for this is that the speed of light is at its maximum only when it is travelling through a vacuum. It slows down when it passes through different mediums. Refraction is a useful property of light that is utilized in lenses for different optical instruments.

A straw in water appears bent because of refraction.

Diffraction

Light does not have the ability to bend around corners the way sound does, but when it passes through any gap in an obstacle, it bends slightly away from the obstacle. This is known as diffraction. The amount of diffraction varies based on the wavelength of the light as well as the width of the gap. Sometimes, a bright ring is visible around the Sun or Moon – this is caused by the diffraction of light by particles in the atmosphere.

Diffraction is responsible for the halo sometimes found around the Moon.

Interference

When you dip your fingers in two adjacent spots in a pond, the ripples that spread out collide and merge to form a different pattern. Light waves also behave in a similar fashion. When two light waves meet, they collide and interfere with one another. This is known as interference. Two light waves can meet and amplify to produce a wave of higher amplitude. This is known as constructive interference. Two light waves can also collide and cancel out to result in destructive interference. When a laser beam is shone on two tiny slits located close to each other, the resultant light is in the form of dark and bright bands. The bright bands are formed by constructive interference and the dark bands through destructive interference. Interference is the phenomenon that results in the coloured rainbow patterns found in soap bubbles.

Interference of light results in the rainbow colours in bubbles.

Scattering

The phenomenon of light getting distributed across a large area as it gets reflected off dust and other particles is known as scattering.

Light can get scattered by dust and other particles in the air.

SHADOWS AND ECLIPSES

Shadow is formed when an object blocks light. Objects are usually classified as opaque, translucent or transparent. Objects that are opaque or translucent can make shadows. An eclipse creates shadows on a much larger scale.

Types of Materials

Materials can be classified into three types based on their ability to allow light to pass through them.

Transparent: Any material that allows almost all the light that shines on it to pass through is said to be transparent. Glass and cellophane sheets are examples of transparent materials.

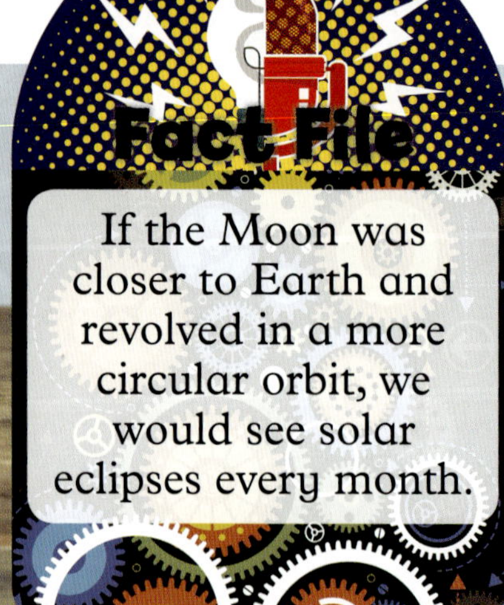
A clear glass is transparent and allows most light to pass through.

A translucent object lets some light pass through.

Translucent: Between transparent and opaque, these materials allow some of the light that strikes them to pass through. Frosted glass and certain plastic materials are translucent. A translucent material such as a piece of sheer fabric will transmit light but cause enough diffusion that objects on the other side of it cannot be seen distinctly.

Opaque: An opaque material blocks all the light that strikes it and forms a distinct shadow. Wood and metals are examples of opaque materials. Light falling on an opaque object is partly absorbed or completely reflected away.

If the Moon was closer to Earth and revolved in a more circular orbit, we would see solar eclipses every month.

A block of wood is opaque and blocks light from passing through it.

Shadow – Umbra and Penumbra

A shadow can be best described as a region where light is missing. Where no light strikes, a dark shadow is formed. It is called 'umbra'. A shadow that forms where some light is allowed and some is blocked is known as penumbra.

If the light source is tiny and concentrated at one point, it forms a sharp shadow. This type of a shadow is called umbra. If the light source is broad and dispersed, a partial shadow called penumbra is formed around the umbra. As the light source moves away from an object, the size and intensity of the shadow also changes.

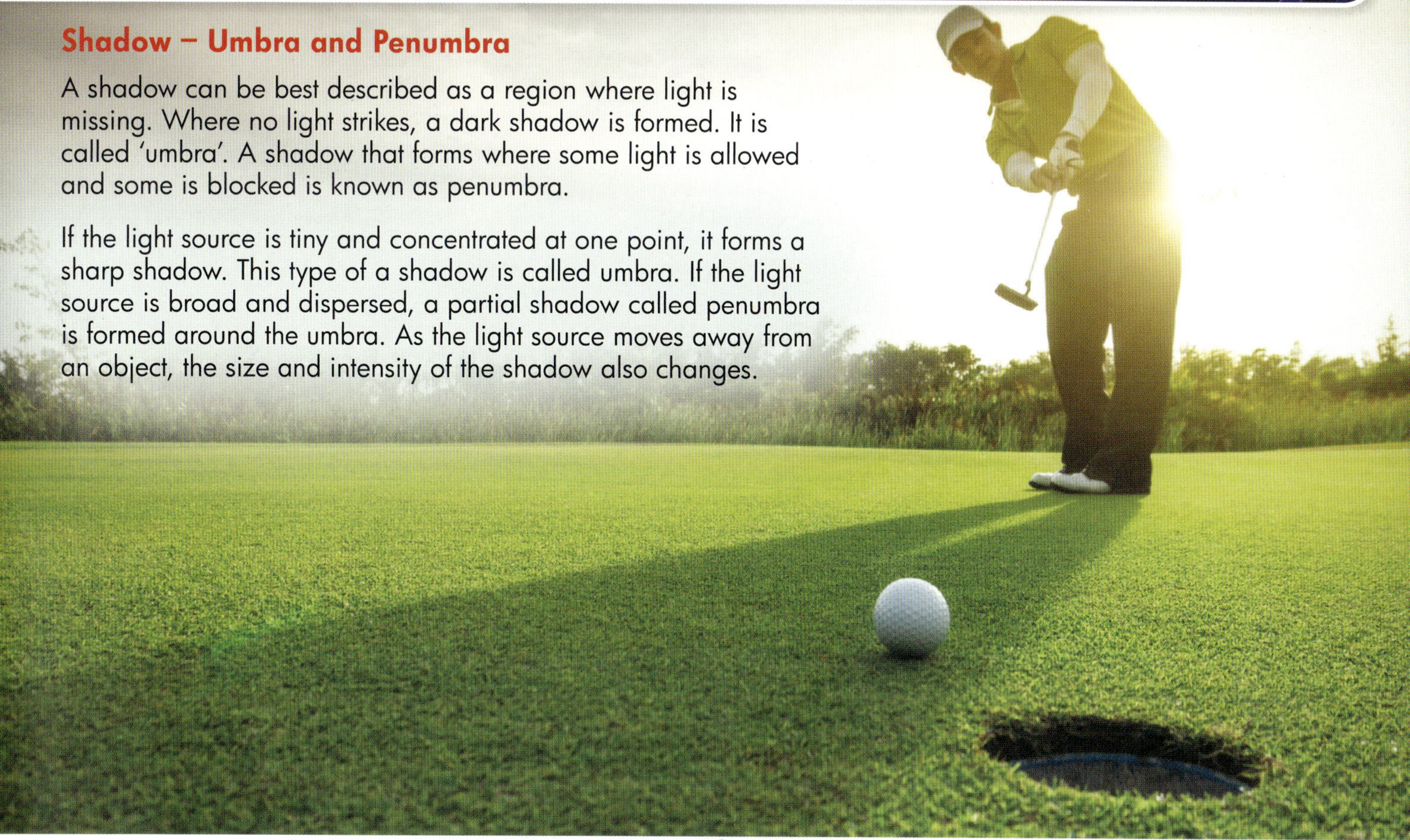

The type of shadow formed depends on the angle of light.

Eclipse

An eclipse occurs when a large planetary body such as the Moon, or another planet, blocks out another by casting its shadow. On Earth, we see two types of eclipses – solar eclipse and lunar eclipse.

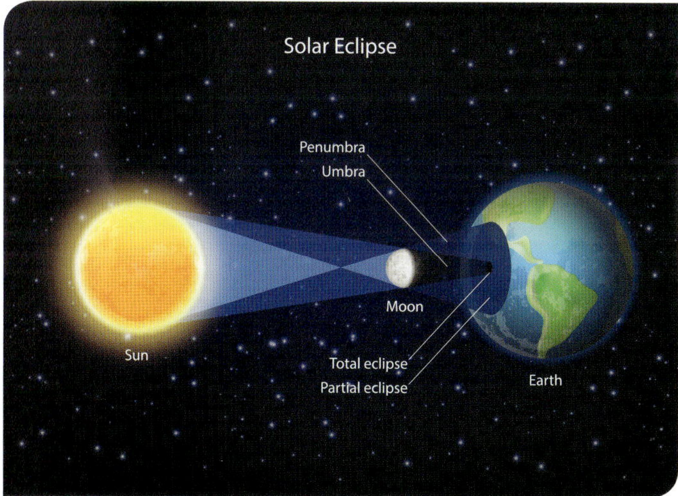

A solar eclipse forms when the Moon comes directly between the Sun and the Earth.

A solar eclipse occurs when the Moon passes in front of the Sun and causes a shadow to fall on certain regions of the Earth. This is the reason why an eclipse can never be viewed from all parts of the Earth, but only where its shadow falls. During an eclipse, in certain locations, it appears as if the Sun has gone dark. A total eclipse is when the Moon completely covers the Sun. A partial eclipse is when only a portion of the Sun is blocked by the Moon. A solar eclipse lasts no longer than seven and a half minutes.

The reason why we are able to see solar eclipses involves the Sun's distance from Earth and its size. The Sun is approximately 400 times the distance between the Earth and the Moon. The Sun's diameter is also roughly 400 times larger than that of the Moon.

A lunar eclipse occurs when the Moon passes behind the Earth and falls into its shadow. The shadow blocks the Sun and results in an eclipse. A lunar eclipse occurs only when the Sun, Earth and Moon are perfectly lined up.

An eclipse usually occurs in phases.

LENSES

A lens is any transparent block made of plastic or glass that is capable of refracting light to form an image. The two common types of lenses are converging and diverging. The amount of light that a lens can refract depends on a measure called its refractive index.

Converging Lens

A converging lens or convex lens is curved on both sides. Light rays coming from an object arrive parallel to one another at the lens. The parallel rays then converge or come together at a point called the principal focus. The distance between the centre of the lens and the point of focus is known as the focal point. Convex lenses are used in magnifying glasses, telescopes, microscopes and binoculars to magnify objects.

A convex lens can concentrate sunlight on one spot.

Diverging Lens

A diverging lens or concave lens is curved inwards on either side. The diverging lens is useful for refracting parallel rays of light and causing them to diverge or spread apart. As a result, only a virtual image is formed that cannot be captured on a screen. The point at which the rays appear to come from is the principal focus. The distance between the centre of the lens and the virtual image is the principal focus. Concave lenses are used in video projectors to enable an image to spread out.

A video projector uses a concave lens.

All lenses, until the 20th century, were made by grinding pieces of glass into different shapes.

Lenses and Ray Diagrams

Ray diagrams are useful for representing the action of converging lenses. A principal axis is drawn through the centre of the lens. The light rays are shown as parallel lines and for the sake of simplicity, only 3 or 4 rays are shown. Any ray that passes parallel to the principal axis gets refracted to a focus behind the lens. A ray passing through the centre of the lens emerges without being refracted. The image forms where the two rays meet. A real image formed from a convex lens is inverted and represented as an arrow. The rays emerging from a concave lens are traced back to get an upright virtual image.

Ray diagrams are useful for identifying:

- If an image is magnified or diminished in size when compared to the original object

- If an image is upright or inverted

- If an image is real or virtual

How Do Lenses Work?

Lenses are transparent pieces of glass or clear plastic that work on the principle of refraction. The light rays that pass through a convex or concave lens change direction. The rays seem to come from a point that is closer or farther away from the original position, thus making them appear smaller or bigger.

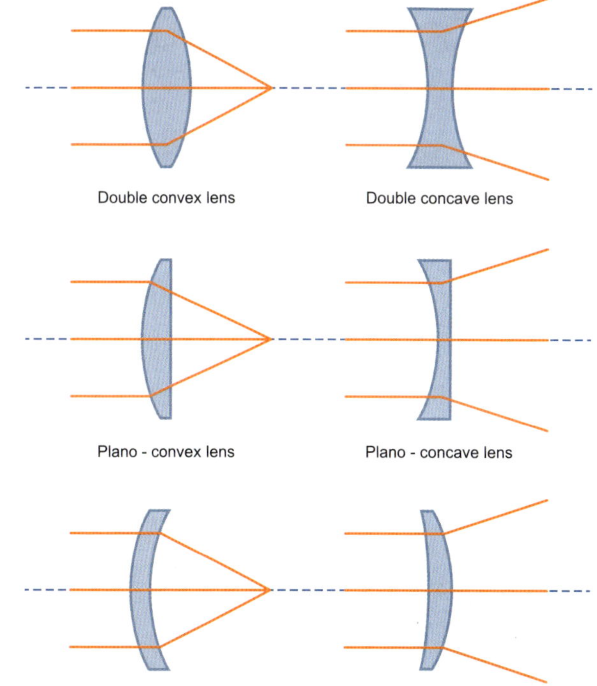

Ray diagrams represent the result of light passing through different lenses.

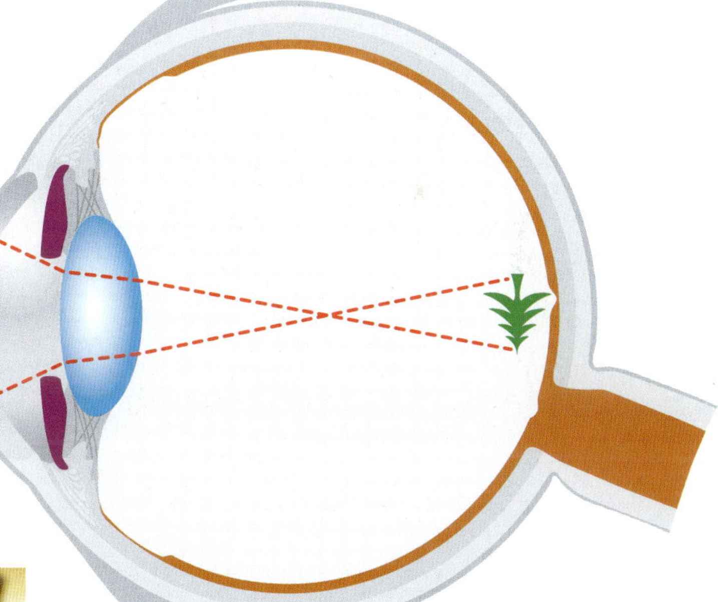

The lens in our eye focuses an image onto the retina, which transmits them to the brain.

Lenses are manufactured with moulds and grinding tools.

How Are Lenses Made?

Convex lenses are made using a concave grinding tool and concave lens are prepared using convex tools. Generally, the glass used for window panes is not suitable for making lenses. The glass that is used for lenses has to be free of air bubbles and any imperfections. An inferior quality glass can cause the lens to produce fuzzy images. The material used for making lenses is known as optical glass. Nowadays, plastic lenses are more common because plastic is cheaper and easier to mould into the desired shape than glass. To increase durability, plastic lenses are often coated with protective materials.

APPLICATION OF LENSES

There are different types of lenses used for different applications. From simple magnifying glasses to complex microscopes, lenses are used in many ways. In the past, lenses were made by manually grinding glass. Nowadays, it is possible to mass-manufacture lenses with moulded automation.

Magnifying Glass

One of the most basic optical devices, a magnifying glass, uses a single lens to view things, which would otherwise be too small to read or see clearly with the naked eye. A converging lens is used in a magnifying glass and magnification is produced by adjusting its position between the eye and the image analyzed.

A magnifying glass can increase the size of images viewed.

A camera uses lenses to capture images.

Camera

A simple camera consists of a single lens positioned in front of any light-sensitive material such as a roll of film or a sensor. A photographic film contains certain chemical properties that enable it to absorb light energy and its colours. In a digital camera, the film is replaced by an electronic sensor that records information in the form of light intensity and colour. The working mechanism in a simple or a digital camera is the same - a single lens forms an image on a light-sensitive detector. Some cameras use multiple lenses, though together they function as a single converging lens.

A pinhole camera or camera obscura is a crude working model of a camera. It consists of a box with a tiny hole through which light can pass through. Light rays from scenery or objects pass through the hole and into the lightproof box. They form an inverted image on the inside surface of the box. This image can be captured as a permanent snapshot if a light-sensitive chemical material is used inside the box.

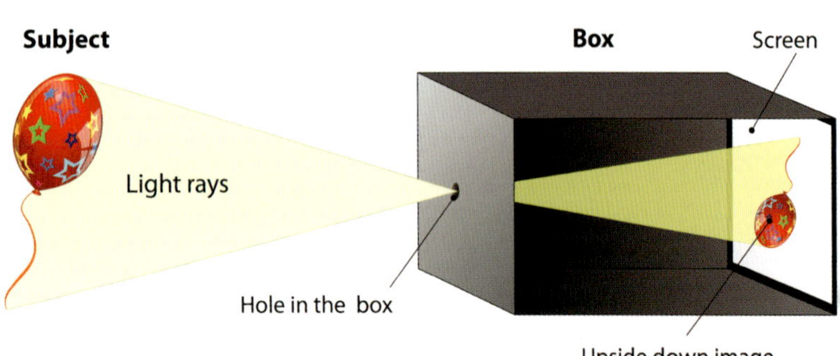

A pinhole camera is a basic working model, and is called a camera obscura.

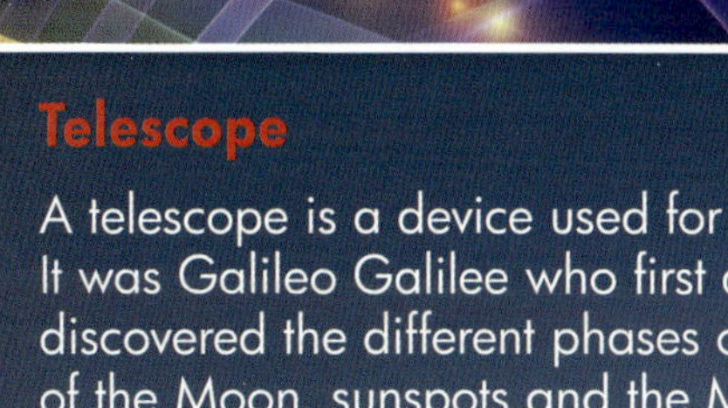

Telescope

A telescope is a device used for magnifying objects that are located at distance. It was Galileo Galilee who first designed a telescope to examine space. He discovered the different phases of Venus, the moons of Jupiter, the cratered surface of the Moon, sunspots and the Milky Way galaxy using this device. A typical telescope consists of two converging lenses at either end of a long tube. The lens facing the object is called the objective and the lens closest to the eye is the eyepiece. The eyepiece magnifies the image produced by the objective lens.

A telescope can be used for observing astronomical objects.

Microscope

A microscope consists of an eyepiece and an objective lens similar to a telescope. Such a setup is also known as a compound microscope. The object to be viewed is placed on a transparent glass slide which in turn is mounted on a platform. This platform is illuminated by natural light using a mirror or artificial light in the form of a lamp. The magnification is achieved by adjusting the lenses for maximum clarity. A compound microscope can provide a maximum magnification of about 100 – 300 times the original size of the object.

An optical microscope is essential in biological laboratories.

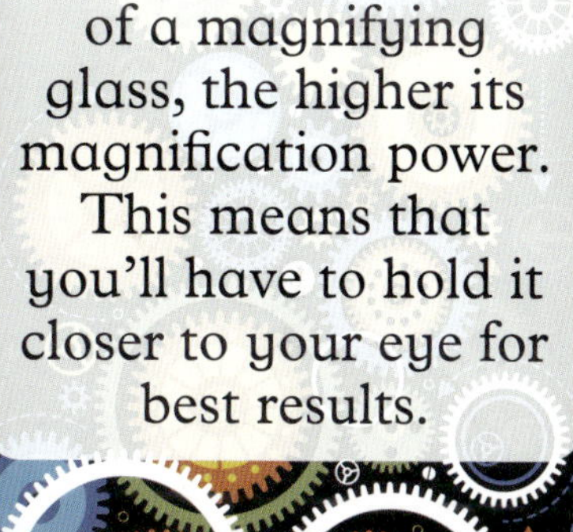

The smaller the lens of a magnifying glass, the higher its magnification power. This means that you'll have to hold it closer to your eye for best results.

LASER

Laser is an artificially produced concentrated light beam that is different from the light emerging from a flashlight or a bulb. The abbreviated term LASER stands for Light Amplification by Stimulated Emission of Radiation. This technology is used in many technological applications and instruments.

LASER – Working Mechanism

Light consists of different wavelengths and even within the visible spectrum there is considerable variation in the wavelengths of colours. White light is actually a mixture of different wavelengths of colours.

A laser beam does not naturally occur in nature. It is produced under specific conditions. A laser beam is a narrow stream of light rays in which all the waves have the same wavelength. Also, all the waves travel in such a way that the crests and troughs of all the waves are perfectly lined up. As a result, they are narrow, very bright and can be focused with intensity on a single spot. Since laser light is focused and does not spread out as much as regular light waves, it can travel across greater distances. Laser beams are capable of concentrating a lot of energy on a very small area.

⊛ Lasers are characterized by a focused and powerful beam of light.

How is Laser Produced?

A laser beam is produced in special glass devices or crystals specifically designed for the purpose. Gases are pumped inside that can absorb energy. The gas atoms get excited and move from an orbit of lower energy to a higher energy orbit. When the atoms return to their stable energy level, the excess energy is released in the form of photons.

The photons that are emitted are all the same wavelength and coherence, with the waves lined up perfectly. The resultant beam of light is narrow, concentrated and a single colour.

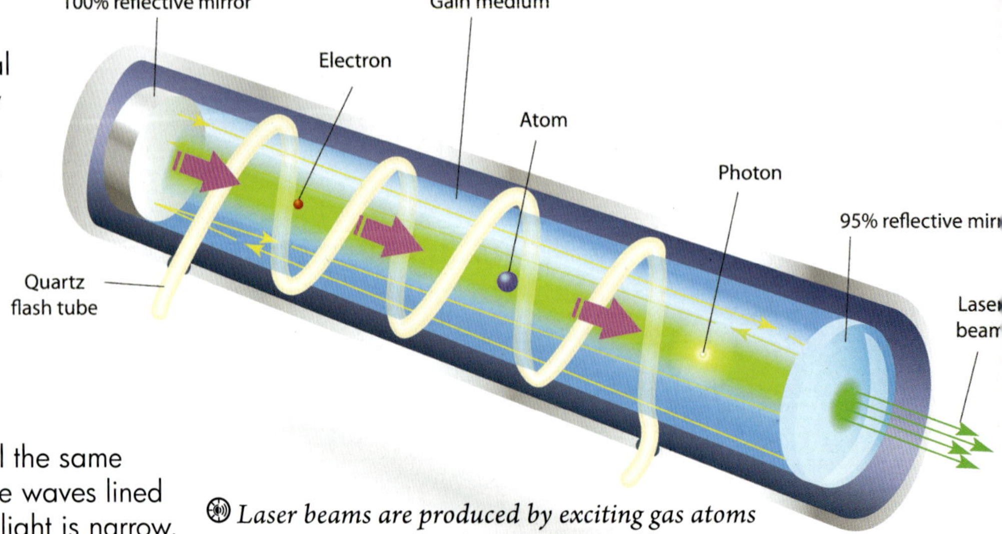

⊛ Laser beams are produced by exciting gas atoms inside specially-designed glass tubes.

Uses of Lasers

Lasers have a wide range of applications.

1. They are useful in precision tools that can cut through tough materials such as diamonds or thick metals.

2. They are used in delicate surgery that needs precise cutting without widespread damage to surrounding tissues.

3. Lasers are used in telecommunication media for recording and retrieving information. They are useful for carrying television and internet signals and data.

Barcode scanners use laser beams.

4. Lasers are the key components of laser printers and barcode scanners.

5. Lasers are also used for designing accurate parts used in computers and certain electronic devices.

6. They are used in scientific instruments called spectrometers, that are used for identifying the chemical nature of samples. The Mars Curiosity Rover used a laser spectrometer to identify the chemicals present in the rocks on the surface.

7. Lasers have been used in studying the gases in the Earth's atmosphere and also in instruments that can map the surfaces of planets, moons and asteroids.

8. Lasers are employed in various research laboratories for studying quantum optics, atomic physics, spectroscopy and plasma studies.

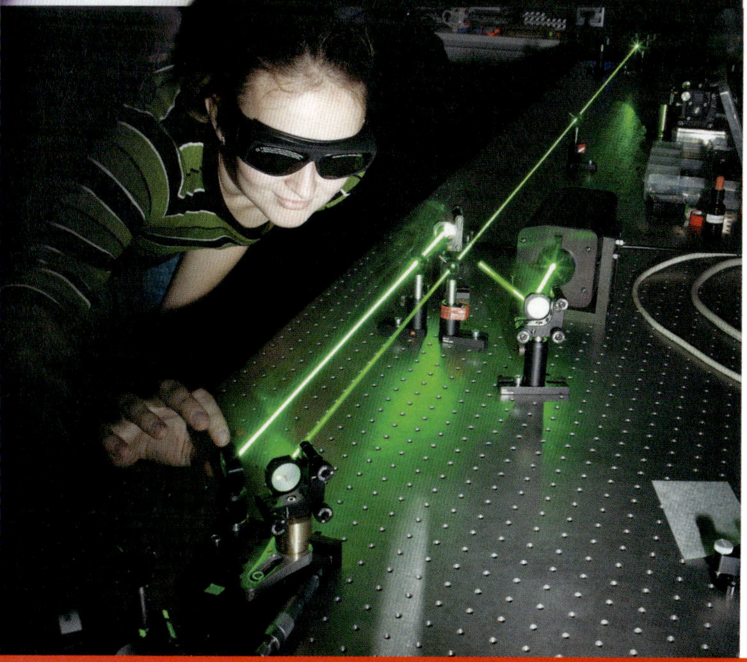

Lasers are used in research laboratories for different studies.

Fact File

The distance between the Earth and Moon has been calculated by identifying the time taken for a laser beam to travel to the Moon and back.

OPTICAL FIBERS

Optical fibres are components used in electronics for carrying information in the form of light or infrared waves. Compared to an ordinary electric cable of the same dimension, an optical fibre cable is capable of carrying more information.

What is an Optical Fibre?

An optical fibre is a thin, transparent rod made of durable and high-quality glass. The glass material absorbs very little light and hence is able to transmit light signals effectively. It is flexible and transparent and no thicker than a human hair. Hundreds of optical fibres are combined to form a cable. They are used in fibre optic communications where transmission over long distances is possible.

Parts of an Optical Fibre

An optical fibre cable is made up of five major parts. The many strands that are bundled together to produce a single channel for light to pass through is called the 'core'. A protective coating or sheath surrounds this structure and is referred to as 'cladding'. This sheath enhances the internal reflection capability of the core thus minimising data loss. Above the sheath, there is another layer of plastic called 'coating' surrounding the core for reinforcement. This layer protects the cable and reduces bending and adds support. This is surrounded by a layer of 'strengthening fibres' that protects the core from excessive stretching and external forces. The last and final layer is known as the 'cable jacket'. It is similar to the plastic sheath found in regular electrical wires and cables. The glass core, which is the only part of the optical fibre which carries light signals, is covered by several layers of protection because it is brittle and prone to damage.

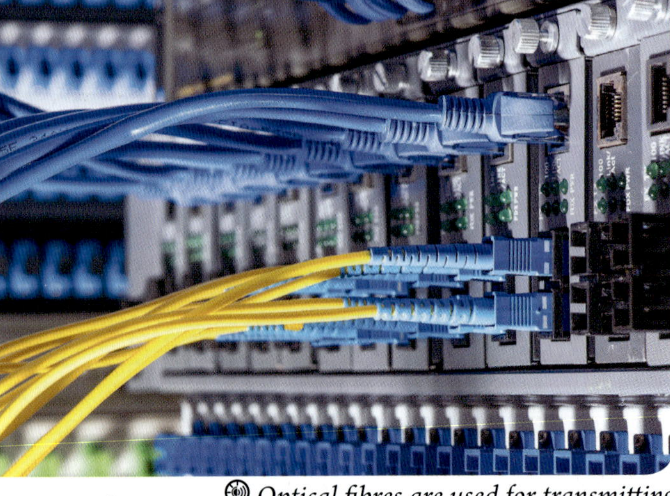

Optical fibres are used for transmitting signals quickly and efficiently.

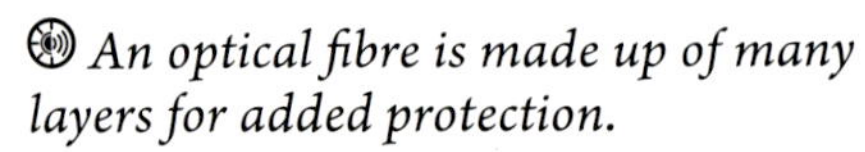

An optical fibre is made up of many layers for added protection.

Total Internal Reflection

Optical fibres work on the principle of total internal reflection. You might have observed that when you switch on a flashlight in a passage, the light emerging from it travels in a straight line. However, if it is possible to place mirrors wherever there are bends in the passage, it is possible to reflect the light across a long distance. This is exactly what an optical fibre achieves but instead of mirrors, it relies on a phenomenon called total internal reflection. The material of the fibre is designed to absorb as little light as possible and to reflect all the light that strikes it.

The light signals received at one end undergo repeated total internal reflection along the fibre and emerge out of the other end. One advantage of optical fibre is that light can be transmitted effectively from one end to the other, even if the fibre is bent. Unlike other ordinary cables, the signal also stays strong over long distances.

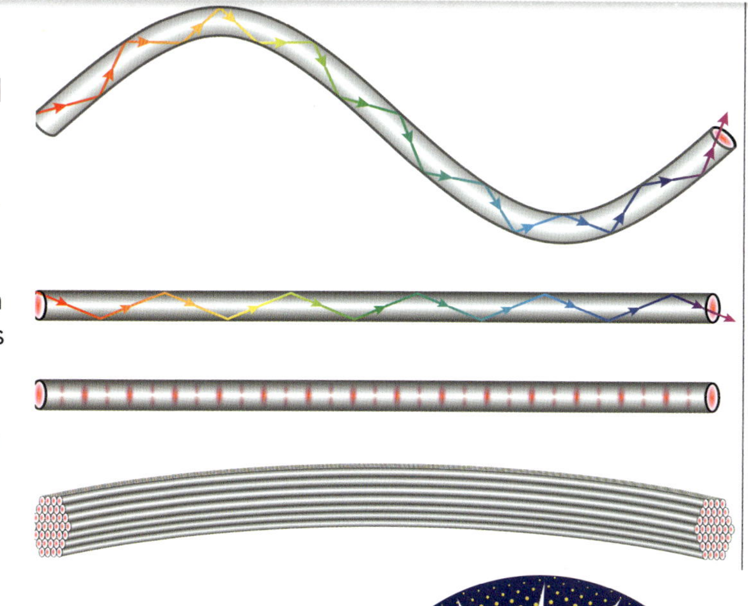

Total internal reflection is the working mechanism behind optical fibres.

Uses

Optical fibres are used for illumination and imaging purposes as well as for wireless internet connection. Specially-designed fibres have a variety of other applications such as optic sensors and lasers. The field of science that deals with design and research in optical fibres and light-mediated information transfer is known as fibre optics.

Fact File

Fibre optic cables do not suffer from electromagnetic interference that metal cable wires are susceptible to.

Optical fibres are used for wireless internet connection.

BLACK BODY

All objects emit and absorb infrared radiation, irrespective of their temperature. The hotter an object is the more infrared radiation it gives out at any given time. It is also true that a very hot object emits radiation, most of which lies in the visible spectrum.

What is a Black Body?

Theoretically, there is no object that can absorb and emit 100% of all the radiation that falls on it. However, there are certain objects that are capable of absorbing or reflecting most of the radiation directed at them. Such an object is called a 'black body'. A black body is the most ideal absorber and radiator of electromagnetic radiation in all wavelengths. The name is derived from the fact that a very cold object that absorbs and emits all incident radiation, appears black in colour.

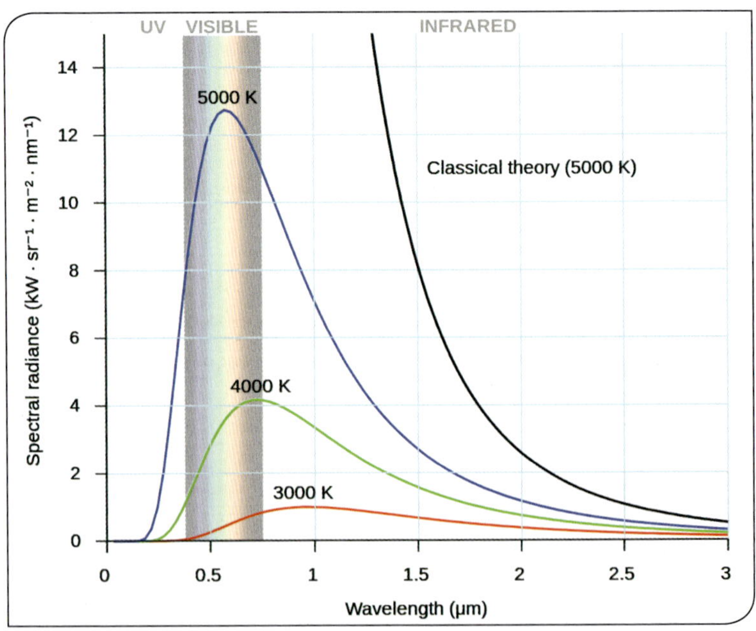

The black body radiation intensity is plotted against wavelength. The hotter a black body, the shorter the wavelength at which intensity is maximum.

Black Body Radiation

The energy emitted by a black body is referred to as black body radiation. The radiation can be plotted on a graph against intensity of radiation and wavelength. The maximum point in the graph line shows the wavelength at which radiation intensity is highest. This factor depends on the temperature of the black body. The hotter the black body is, the shorter the wavelength at which radiation is most intense.

Scientists have used a measure of the black body radiation to determine the temperatures of objects in space. The calculations are made based on the assumption that celestial objects such as stars behave as perfect black bodies, even though they are theoretically not. However, several astronomical objects come very close to this ideal condition. One of the best examples of a naturally-occurring black body is a star. Stars can emit light at different wavelengths and also absorb radiation.

Generally, white and silvery surfaces are the poorest absorbers of radiation. They reflect back nearly all visible light that strikes them.

Objects that are poor absorbers are also poor emitters. They do not emit radiation as quickly as darker colours. This is why radiators in homes are usually painted white in colour. This way, they emit infrared radiation more slowly and gradually.

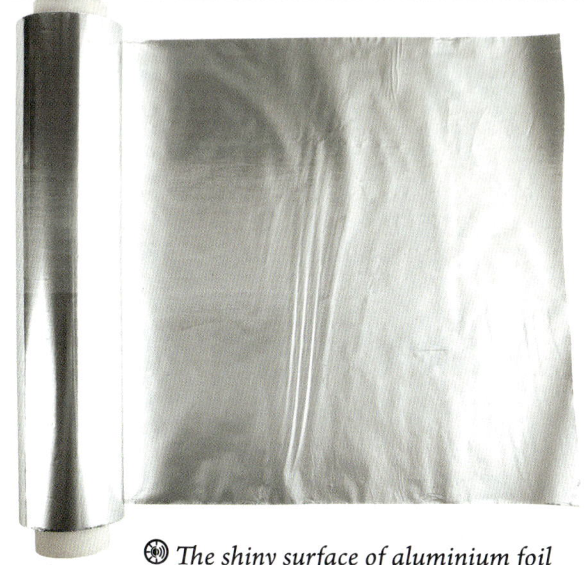

The shiny surface of aluminium foil reflects back most light striking it.

Home radiators are often coloured white to reduce emission of radiation.

Near Black Materials

Research in black bodies is useful for designing materials that can be used for camouflage and radar invisibility. These materials can also be used in telescopes and cameras to provide anti-reflective surfaces that reduce stray light and improve contrast. One such substance that is capable of transforming any object to being nearly black, is called lamp black.

A practical example of a black body is a small hole punched through a box coated with lamp black. The lamp black coating ensures that at least 97% of the incident light is absorbed.

Black Hole

A black hole is considered to be a nearly perfect black body because it consists of a region of space through which nothing escapes, not even light. The region around a black hole is referred to as an 'event horizon'. The black hole absorbs all the light that hits the horizon and reflects back almost nothing. The cosmic microwave background radiation that we observe in space is an example of black body radiation. Black body radiation that is predicted to be released from a black hole is referred to as Hawking radiation, named after Stephen Hawking who described the phenomenon. A black hole will continue to emit radiation until it exhausts its energy completely.

A black hole is an example of a nearly perfect black body.

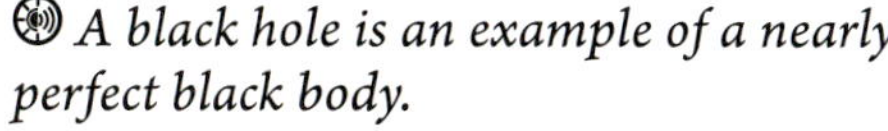

RADIATION AND EARTH

Different objects have different temperatures which are linked to the balance between absorbed and emitted radiation. Any object that emits a greater amount of radiation tends to be hotter and one that emits less has a lower temperature. Earth's average temperature is decided by a number of factors.

The Sun is the source of electromagnetic radiation received on Earth.

Solar Radiation

The Sun is the main source of radiation and energy on Earth. The Sun's solar radiation spectrum is similar to that of a nearly perfect black body. The Sun emits radiation across the electromagnetic spectrum which includes visible light, infrared radiation, ultraviolet rays, X-rays and radio waves.

The constant nuclear fusion reaction inside the Sun also produces high energy gamma rays. However, by the time they reach the surface of the Sun they have lost most of their energy and are reabsorbed. Gamma rays are emitted only in solar flares. The amount of solar radiation received by planets is inversely proportional to the distance – the closer a planet is to the Sun, the more radiation it will experience.

Gamma rays are emitted during solar flares.

Factors Affecting Earth's Temperature

The Earth has a thick atmosphere that protects the organisms on the surface from the harmful ultraviolet rays and infrared radiation. Ultraviolet rays are absorbed by the ozone layer in the troposphere layer of the atmosphere. The absorbed radiation is emitted back as heat into the stratosphere layer above. Some of the heat is also radiated back into outer space beyond the atmosphere. The rest of the heat is sent back to the Earth's surface.

The temperature of Earth depends on the gases present in the atmosphere and their ability to absorb and retain radiation. The Earth has three major gases that absorb visible and infrared radiation. They are water vapor, carbon dioxide and methane. These are referred to as 'greenhouse gases'. The average temperature of Earth is decided by the amount absorbed and the amount emitted by the surface and the atmosphere.

The ozone layer offers protection against ultraviolet rays.

Effect of Radiation

Whenever the Earth's surface absorbs visible and infrared radiation, the internal energy increases and the surface grows hotter. A part of the energy is transferred to the atmosphere through conduction and convection.

Earth also radiates infrared radiation, some of which is transmitted across the atmosphere back into space. The greenhouse gases present in the atmosphere emit infrared radiation in all directions, including the Earth's surface and outer space. This activity is important for stabilising the average temperature of the planet.

Pollution has been a major factor in causing global warming.

Global warming results in the melting of polar ice caps and glaciers.

Human activities such as fossil fuel burning and deforestation are causing an increased release of carbon dioxide into the atmosphere. Since carbon dioxide is a greenhouse gas, it traps and reabsorbs radiation; a phenomenon that leads to climate change.

Rising global temperatures resulting from climate change will eventually have a disastrous effect on organisms. Polar regions are particularly susceptible to melting as a result of global warming and will affect coastal regions throughout the world, as well as drastically changing climate patterns. By the end of this century, several islands will be at risk of sinking below sea level.

Scientists have observed that during solar flares, the Sun emits X-rays.

SOUND

Our world is filled with many different sounds at any point in time. Sound is a type of mechanical wave that is formed by the vibration of particles moving through a medium. The vibrations are detected as sound by an auditory system. One important feature of sound is that it needs a medium to be transmitted.

Longitudinal Waves

Sound is an example of longitudinal wave. When sound waves move in a particular direction, particles of air are displaced on either side, responding to the transport of energy. As a result of the longitudinal motion of the particles, certain regions of the air are compressed and other regions spread apart. They are referred to as compressions and rarefactions respectively. Compressions have high air pressure and rarefactions have low air pressure.

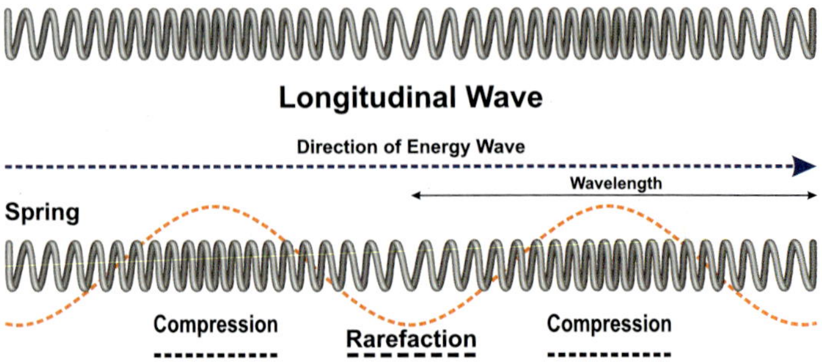

Sound travels in the form of longitudinal waves.

Medium for Sound

A wave is a disturbance that is transported from one location to another through a medium. A medium is any material consisting of particles that can transmit the vibrations. The medium can be air, water or metal.

If you shout or play an instrument in space, it is impossible to hear it. This is because space is just a vacuum, and sound cannot be transmitted in the absence of interacting particles. A sound wave gets transmitted through particle-to-particle interaction, and hence is known as a mechanical wave.

Sound can only travel in the presence of a medium, like air.

Ultrasound and Infrasound

The human ear can typically hear frequencies of 20 to 20,000 Hertz. There are other animals that can hear sounds of frequencies lower or higher than this range. An example is the dog whistle which is audible to dogs, but not to humans. This is because the sound produced by the whistle is at a frequency higher than 20,000 Hertz.

Ultrasound refers to sound waves that have frequencies higher than the upper limit of human audibility, greater than 20,000 Hertz.

Bats naturally emit ultrasonic waves and listen to echoes to find their way. This is known as echolocation. Infrasound is sound wave with frequency lower than 20 Hertz. Whales, elephants and certain other animals can hear infrasound.

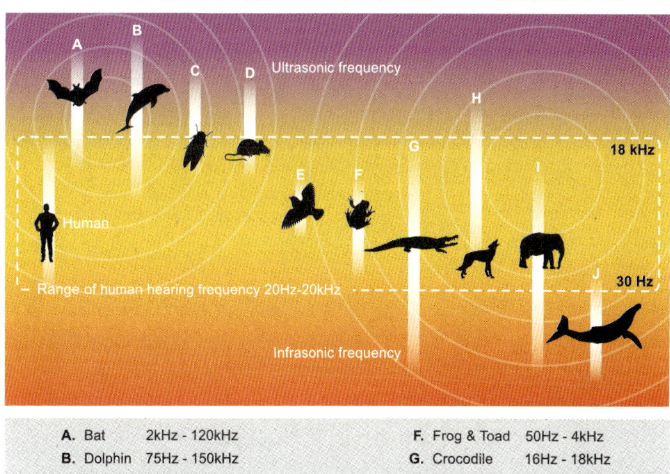

A.	Bat	2kHz - 120kHz		F.	Frog & Toad	50Hz - 4kHz
B.	Dolphin	75Hz - 150kHz		G.	Crocodile	16Hz - 18kHz
C.	Insect	10kHz - 80kHz		H.	Dog	64Hz - 44kHz
D.	Rat	900Hz - 79kHz		I.	Elephant	17Hz - 10.5kHz
E.	Bird	1kHz - 4kHz		J.	Blue whale	14Hz - 36Hz

Different animal species can perceive sounds of varying frequency ranges.

There are applications for ultrasonic and infrasonic waves. Ultrasonic waves are used in ultrasound scans for medical diagnosis and sonograms. Submarines and ships send and receive ultrasonic waves to guide them through the water and to detect other ships and objects nearby. Infrasonic waves are used for detecting volcanic eruptions.

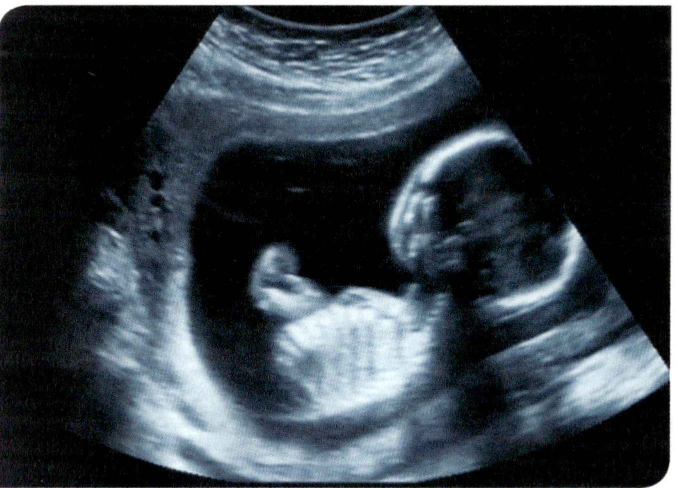

Ultrasound technology is used for medical diagnosis.

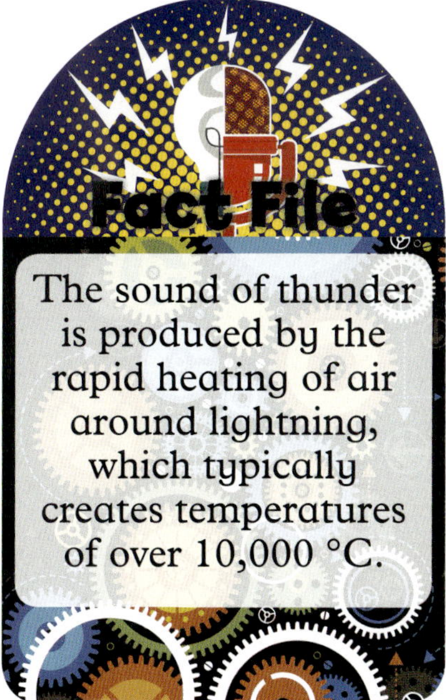

A soundproof room is essential for high quality audio and music recording.

Sound-Proofing

A space is said to be sound-proof if it does not allow sound waves to penetrate inside ir. It is important to have sound-proof rooms for recording music or audio. Such a room would filter out all external noise and provide the right environment for a clear recording. Sound-proofing is achieved by one of these three ways:

1. Using a material that can absorb sound

2. Creating a two-structured space, one structure separated from the other, so that sound can penetrate only the first structure and not travel to the second

3. Building a structure of material with more thickness than usual so that sound is reflected away or converted into another form of energy.

PROPERTIES OF SOUND

Sound waves are similar to light waves and share some characteristic features that are common to all waves. It is possible to measure speed, wavelength, frequency and amplitude of sound waves. Sound also exhibits properties such as reflection, refraction, absorption and diffraction.

Characteristic Features of Sound Waves

Speed: The distance traveled by sound in a given time is calculated as its speed. The speed of sound is 340 metres per second at 15 degrees Celsius. You might note that the speed of sound is much lower than the speed of light. It is the reason why lightning is seen before the accompanying thunder is heard.

Certain aircraft and land-based vehicles can travel at speeds exceeding the speed of sound. A white cloud forms around aircraft that travel at supersonic speed.

Whenever there is a change in temperature, the speed of sound changes. Sound travels faster in solids than in liquids and gases. This is because the particles making up a solid are closely packed and transmit sound more efficiently.

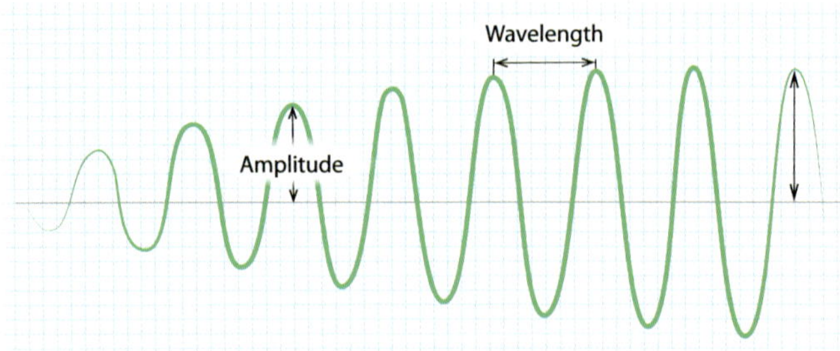

⊛ *The amplitude of sound gives information about its loudness*

⊛*As sound travels slower than light, thunder is heard only after lightning is seen.*

⊛ *Certain aircraft can travel faster than sound.*

Wavelength: The distance between two consecutive crests or troughs is measured as the wavelength.

Frequency: The number of waves passing through any point per second is known as the frequency.

Amplitude: The fluctuation of a wave from its mean value is measured as the amplitude. In the case of sound waves, it refers to the extent to which the particles of a medium are displaced due to the vibrations. Amplitude is useful for measuring the loudness of sound.

Pitch: It is a measure of the frequency of a sound characterising how high or low it is. It also determines the quality of sound. It is calculated in cycles/second.

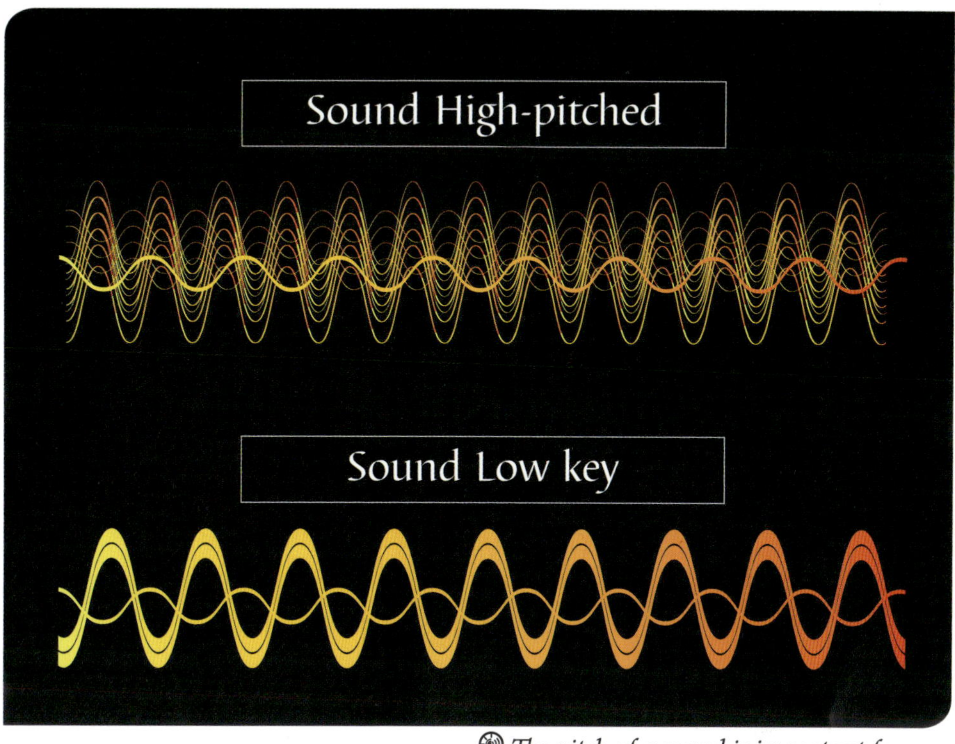

The pitch of a sound is important for assessing the quality

Physical Properties

Like light, sound waves also experience certain phenomena unique to waves.

Reflection

Like other waves, sound also undergoes reflection when it travels from one medium to another. In sound, the phenomenon of reflection can result in one of two results – echo or reverberation. Reverberation happens in an area of smaller height and length, not exceeding 17 metres in distance. Echo is the same as reverberation, but occurs when the reflected sound wave reaches the ear a millisecond (0.1 second) after we hear the original sound.

Refraction

Refraction is the process by which there is a change in the direction of sound waves as they move from one medium to another. Along with the bending of waves, there is also a change in the speed and wavelength. So, when sound waves travel from air to water, the speed, velocity, wavelength and direction of the wave changes as a result of refraction.

Absorption

Whenever sound waves strike upon any surface, part of the energy gets scattered and part of it is absorbed. Absorption is the phenomenon by which the energy of sound waves transforms from one form to another. Generally, high frequency sound waves are absorbed more readily than low frequency waves.

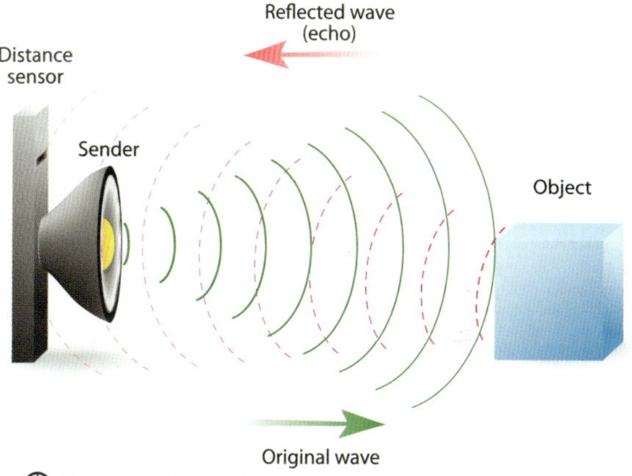

Echo and reverberation are phenomena caused by sound reflection

Like light, sound waves also undergo refraction

Diffraction

Diffraction is the bending and change in direction of sound waves when encountering obstacles. The amount of diffraction increases with an increase in wavelength of sound waves. Diffraction is observed when sound waves pass through a barrier with small openings.

PHYSICS OF HEARING

Hearing is the perception of sound. By listening to any sound, one can gather a lot of information such as the direction from which it is emitted, its pitch and loudness. It is also possible to detect the quality of sound such as whether it is pleasant or harsh. The ears are the human organs responsible for hearing.

Hearing Range

Humans have a hearing range of 20 – 20,000 Hertz. Sounds below and above this range are inaudible. Infrasound, below 20 Hertz cannot be heard but can be felt as vibration. A few people are capable of hearing ultrasound slightly above 20,000 Hertz.

The perception of frequency of sound is referred to as pitch. Generally, children can perceive high-pitched sounds better than adults as the perception power reduces with age. Even though we cannot perceive ultrasound, we can produce it using electricity or magnetism.

Dogs can hear sounds with frequencies of up to 30,000 Hertz. Bats and dolphins can perceive sounds as high as 100,000 Hertz. Elephants can hear sounds under 20 Hertz.

Infrasound
(below 16 Hz)

Audible frequencies
(16 Hz - 20kHz)

Ultrasound
(over 20 kHz)

Measuring Sound

The rate at which sound reaches a certain area is defined as the sound intensity. Since the human ear can detect a large range of sound (20 – 20,000 Hertz), we use a logarithmic scale to measure sound waves.

The term 'decibel' is used to measure sound based on the increase in pressure. For instance, when the pressure of a sound wave doubles, it corresponds to a 6 decibel increase. It is abbreviated as 'dB'.

Phon is another measure of sound. It is roughly equivalent to 1000 decibels. It is a measure of individual perception of loudness. The difference between 'phon' and 'decibel' is that while the former is a measure of loudness perception, the latter is a measure of sound intensity.

⊛ Sounds below and above the audible range of humans are called infrasound and ultrasound.

Sone is another scale that calculates loudness. A 10 phon increase in a sound will correspond to a doubling of the loudness. The loudness of 1 sone is equivalent to the loudness of a 40 phon sound.

Here are a few examples of sounds and their corresponding measured decibels:

180 dB: Rocket during lift-off

140 dB: Jet engine during take-off

120 dB: A loud rock band

110 dB: Thunder

90 dB: Regular traffic in a busy city

80 dB: Loud radio or music

60 dB: Regular conversation

30 dB: Soft whispers

0 dB: Lowest/softest sound audible to human ear

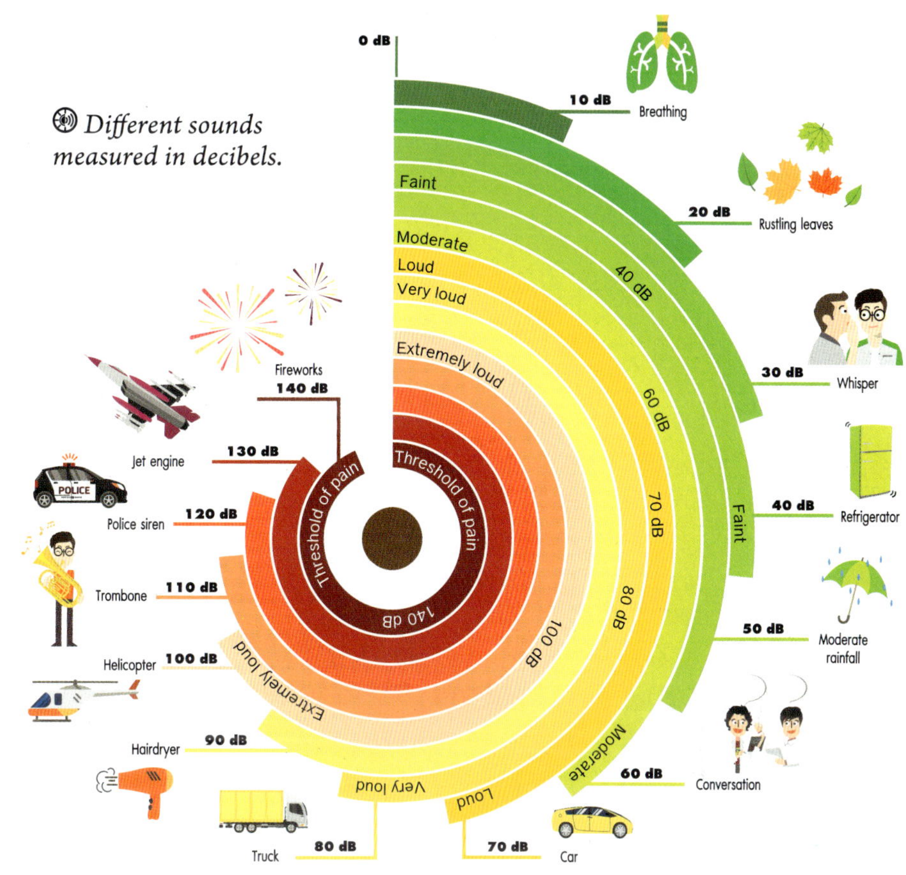

Different sounds measured in decibels.

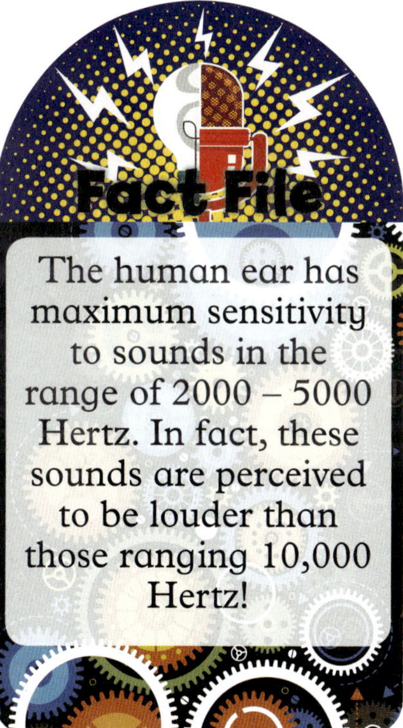

Sound in the Ears

Sound enters into the ear through the narrow passage leading to the ear drum. The ear drum vibrates when the sound waves strike. The vibrations are then transmitted to the three tiny bones located in the middle ear. The function of these bones is to amplify the sound vibrations and send them to a fluid-filled structure called cochlea. The vibrations cause a rippling effect and stimulate the movement of hair cells which in turn cause a release of chemicals and the transmission of an electrical signal to the brain for perception.

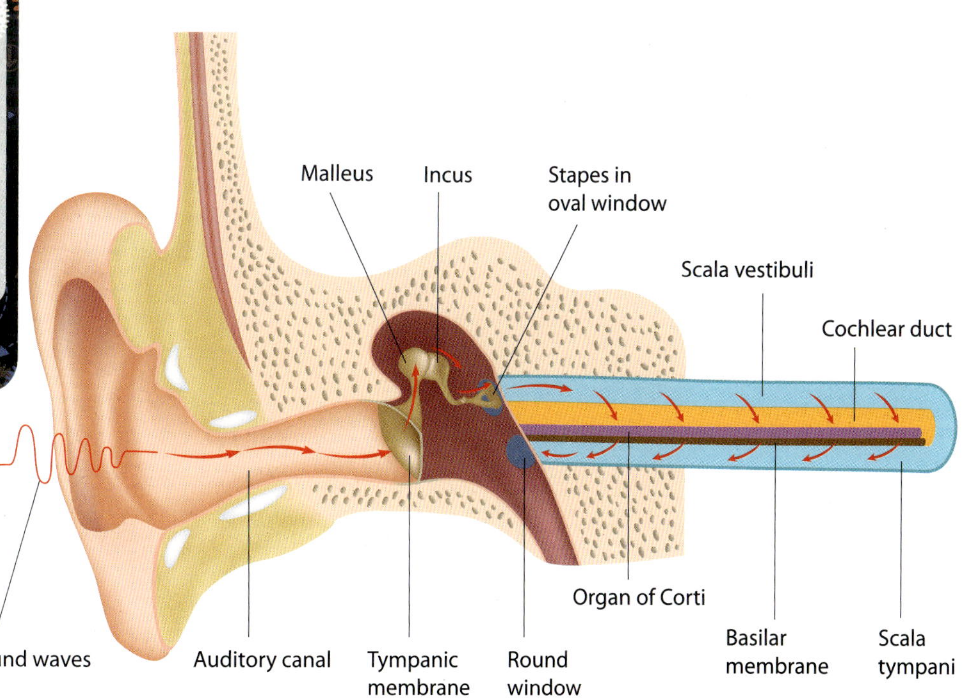

The ear has many parts that collect and transmit sound.

MOTION

Motion is the activity or movement involved in changing the position of a body. The study of motion is known as mechanics. The study of motion and its forces is known as dynamics. There are different types of motion. They are – random, translational, rotational and oscillatory motion.

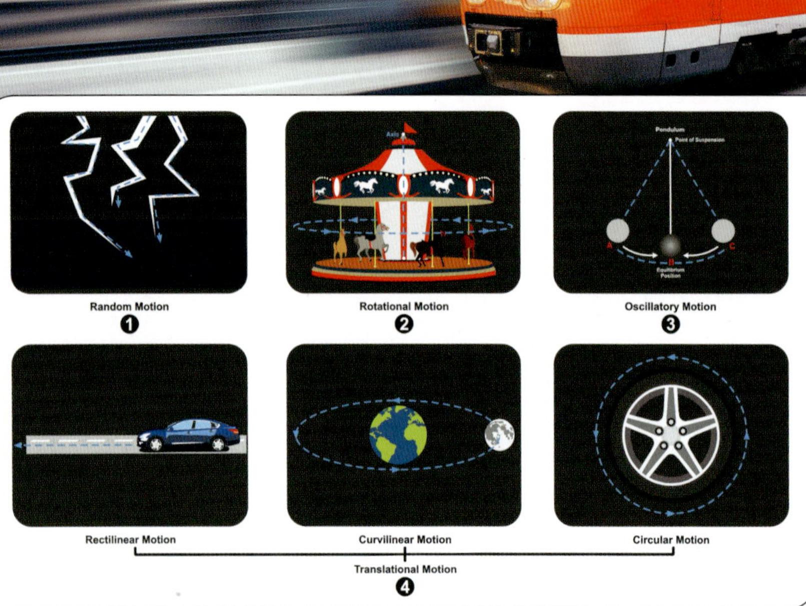

Motion can be classified into different types.

What is Motion?

We live in a universe filled with particles, atoms and molecules that are always in motion. The planets are revolving around the Sun and the solar system in turn is rushing through space. At the atomic level, the electrons are constantly and ceaselessly revolving around the nucleus. Motion can be uniform or uneven. Uniform motion is the movement of an object along a straight line. Uneven motion is the movement along a path that cannot be predicted or accurately measured.

Fact File

Light moves at the speed of 299,792 kilometres per second. The light from the Sun takes approximately 8 minutes to reach the Earth.

A stone thrown in the air describes curvilinear motion.

Translational Motion

The type of motion that results in a change of location along a linear path is known as translational motion. A rolling ball, a bullet fired from a gun, a car moving on the road and a cyclist riding along a straight path are all examples of translational motion. Even though it appears as if translational motion involves only objects moving in a straight line, it also includes motion along a curved path. The latter is referred to as curvilinear motion. A car reversing around a corner, or a stone flung at an angle are examples of curvilinear motion.

Rotational Motion

This type of motion occurs when an object moves about a central axis and different parts of it move by different distances at a given time. A merry-go-round, blades of a fan and a windmill are examples of this motion. The central axis around which an object rotates is referred to as the axis of rotation. While linear motion is measured by a change in position, rotational motion is measured as a change in angle.

A paper windmill exhibits rotational motion.

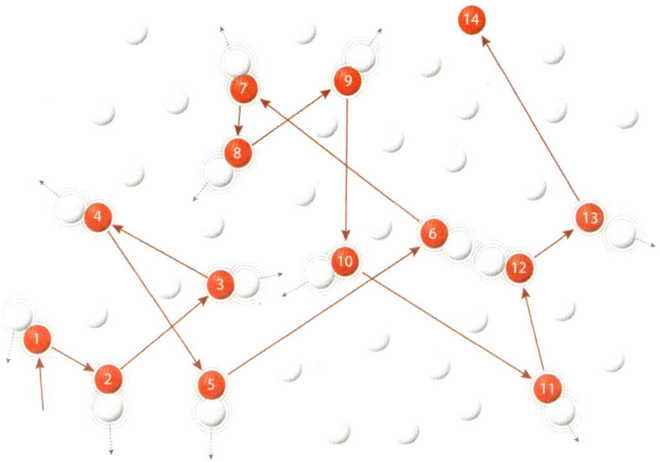

Random motion of particles is also called Brownian motion.

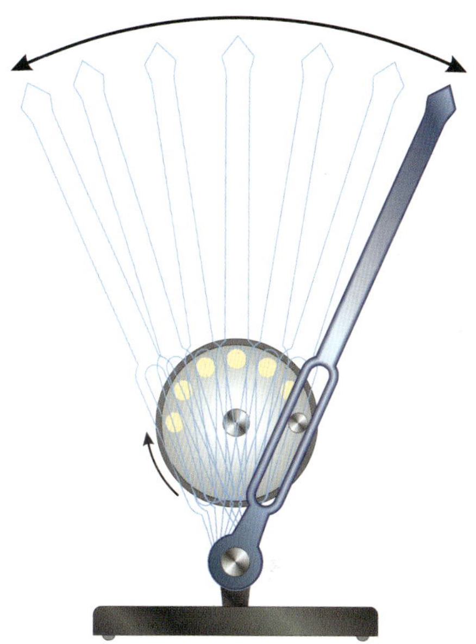

An oscillating lever exhibits oscillatory motion.

Random Motion

Not all types of motion that occur in nature are uniform or periodic. Random motion, also called non-periodic motion, is unpredictable. It is impossible to predict the position of a randomly-moving object at any given time. Molecules of gas move around freely and collide with other molecules they encounter. Similarly, the motion of electrons in atoms is also unpredictable. Brownian motion, which is the movement of particles in a fluid as they collide with each other, is a classic example of random motion.

Oscillatory Motion

This is a repetitive and fluctuating motion between two locations. The classic example of oscillatory motion is the pendulum. Oscillatory motion is periodic in nature. The time taken to complete one cycle or a complete oscillation is measured as a 'period'. Study of periodic motion is important in physics, especially with respect to waves and electromagnetic radiation.

Relativity

Motion of regular objects can be predicted with the help of the three laws of motion proposed by the English physicist, Isaac Newton. These laws are not applicable for very tiny particles moving at tremendous speeds. Motion approaching the speed of light is described using the theory of relativity proposed by another prominent scientist, Albert Einstein. In microscopic bodies, the wave properties of light are also taken into consideration. All types of motions are considered relative, that is, they are perceived differently based on the motion of the observer.

Albert Einstein is credited for the theory of relativity.

FORCES AND MOTION

Force is defined as any 'pushing' or 'pulling' action that causes objects to move, change direction or change shape. According to the Law of Inertia, a body in motion or rest remains in its state until an external force acts upon it. Forces play a key role in the motion of objects.

Effect of Forces on Motion

Forces act on an object to encourage movement, make it move faster or to change its direction. Due to inertia, it is enough to apply an initial force to get an object moving. For instance, a rocket needs force to help it lift off and escape Earth's gravitational pull. Once that is achieved, it will continue in its state of motion until another force acts on it to stop it.

When we look at the motion of objects, it is easy to identify the type of force applied. For instance, when a ball is flung up into the sky and comes down within seconds, we know that it is Earth's gravitational pull that is dragging it down. A rolling ball eventually grinds to a halt because frictional force acts upon it to slow it down.

Pulling and pushing are two common types of forces.

In almost all cases, more than one force is acting on an object at any given time. Sometimes, there are many different forces acting in different directions to exert pull or push. Other times, all the forces add up to one massive overall force.

There are also situations where the forces cancel out and are perfectly in balance. A suspension bridge is an example of balanced forces. The gravity and the weight of the vehicles passing through it at any given time are balanced by the pulling force (called tension) of the suspension cables.

A suspension bridge is balanced by gravity and the tension of cables.

Types of Forces

There are many types of forces. Listed below are a few of them:

Centripetal Force: Any force that acts on a body moving in a circle is known as centripetal force and is directed towards the centre.

Centrifugal Force: Force acting on a body moving in a circle, but directed away from the centre.

Gravitational Force: The pulling force exerted by massive bodies such as stars, planets and moons on other objects with lower mass.

Gravitational force acts on all objects on Earth.

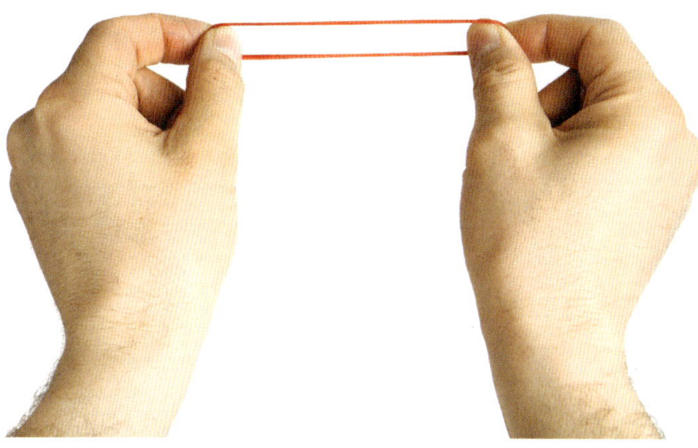

A swinging ball experiences centripetal force.

Elastic force acts to bring the rubber band back to its original shape after stretching.

Tension: Force acting upon an object to stretch it.

Air Resistance: The force exerted by the air on a moving object to slow it down is known as air resistance.

Friction: The force generated when two surfaces interact and slide against each other.

Elastic Force: The force acting on elastic materials such as foam or rubber acting to bring them back to their original shape.

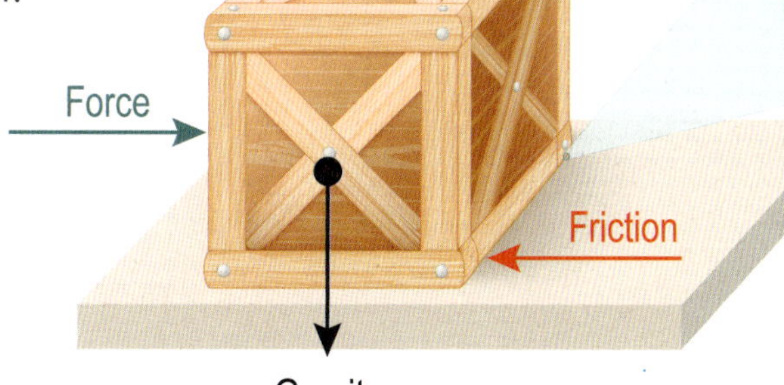

Friction occurs when two surfaces come in contact with each other.

Improving Force

It is possible to increase the forces applied to an object by using levers, pulleys, wheels, gears and ramps. These devices are referred to as 'simple machines'. Even though we have limited physical abilities, using a combination of simple machines can help achieve many seemingly impossible tasks. Industrial machines such as diggers, cranes, bulldozers and harvesters are capable of performing a wide range of tasks quickly and efficiently. Almost all of these machines are equipped with powerful hydraulic arms (liquid-filled cylinders) with attached diggers or other accessories that can do jobs with ease.

SPEED, VELOCITY AND ACCELERATION

Motion is defined by different properties like speed, velocity, acceleration and momentum. The speed is the most basic measure of motion – it records the time taken to travel a specific distance.

Velocity

The rate of change of motion in a particular direction is known as velocity. While speed is also a measure of motion, it does not take direction into consideration. Speed does not convey all the information about a body's motion, but velocity does. Velocity is a more useful measure since it includes direction and you will know in which direction a body moved.

Instantaneous velocity is defined as a measure of speed and direction in a split second. On the outset, it might seem like this is not an important value to measure, but it is useful in accurately measuring average velocity. For instance, if you are calculating the average velocity of a car travelling from one place to another, the instantaneous velocity while it is stuck in a traffic jam is also taken into consideration.

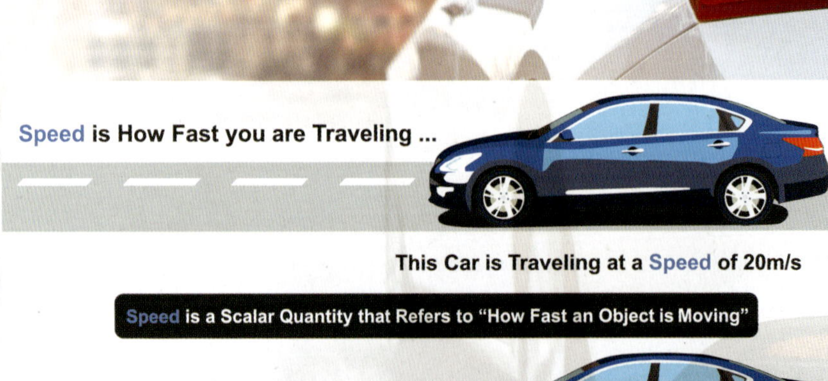

Speed denotes how fast one travels while velocity also gives direction.

Acceleration

The rate of change of velocity is known as acceleration. A body is said to be accelerating if it changes its speed or its direction or both. A plane moving in along a straight line with a constant velocity has zero acceleration. However, if it swoops down and lands, it is said to be accelerating because it has changed speed or direction. When there is a decrease in velocity, it is known as negative acceleration.

An airplane that is about to land has negative acceleration.

Constant acceleration is experienced when there is a constant net force being applied. Gravity is the best example of this phenomenon. Gravity causes a constant pull on the objects on Earth towards the centre.

Momentum

An object that is said to be gaining momentum is something that is in motion with its speed increasing. The more momentum an object gains, the more difficult it is to apply enough force to stop it. Momentum defines the quantity of any object in motion, measured as the product of its mass and velocity. It was the French scientist, Descartes, who first described momentum.

Momentum measures both direction and mass. If there are many particles making up a system, the net momentum of the system is equal to the sum of momentums of all particles. In terms of equation, momentum is the product of an object's mass and velocity.

Escape Velocity

The escape velocity is defined as the speed at which an object needs to travel to escape the gravitational pull of a massive body such as a planet or moon. The escape velocity is closely related to the mass of the planet or moon. This is because the more massive a body is, the more powerful is its gravitational pull. A rocket that is blasting off the Moon's surface can travel at a slower speed than one taking off from Earth. Jupiter is several times more massive than Earth, has more powerful gravity and hence a higher escape velocity.

Fact File

An object shooting out of Earth should travel at a speed of about 25,000 miles per hour to avoid falling back to the surface or stay in an orbit.

NEWTON'S LAWS OF MOTION

The English physicist and mathematician, Isaac Newton, proposed three laws of motion and gravitation that described the functioning of the physical universe. Even though quantum physics has replaced Newton's laws while describing atoms and sub-atomic particles, these laws hold true for all large bodies.

▲ *Isaac Newton was among the most influential physicists in the world.*

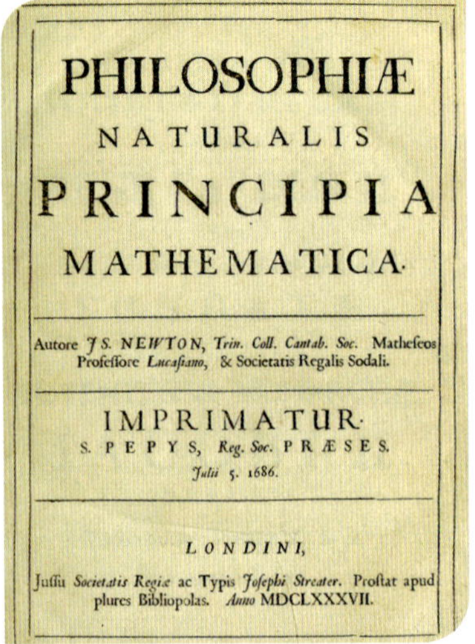

◉ *Newton published his laws in a book referred to simply as 'Principia'.*

The Principia

Considered to be one of the most influential scientists in the world, Isaac Newton was a polymath with a keen interest in mathematics, astronomy, and physics. His work, consisting of three books, is called 'Mathematical Principles of Natural Philosophy'. Originally written in Latin, and simply referred to as 'Principia', it contains his work on gravitation and classic laws of motion concerning large objects. It is considered to be one of the most valuable works in the history of science.

Isaac Newton formulated a set of laws of motion to explain the motion of planets, comets, tides and other physical phenomena. His laws helped conclusively confirm the heliocentric model of the solar system. Newton's laws have been verified independently by several scientists and found to hold true in all cases.

Newton's First Law of Motion

The first law of motion states that: Every object in a uniform state of motion or rest tends to remain in that state unless an external, unbalanced force is applied to it.

This law is similar to Galileo Galilee's concept of inertia, which was known as 'Law of Inertia'. According to Newton's first law, objects are incapable of starting, stopping or changing motion without the application of an external force. A pebble sliding on a frozen lake eventually comes to a stop when frictional force acts on it.

An object at rest stays at rest.

An object acted upon by an unbalanced force changes speed and direction.

An object in motion stays in motion.

An object acted upon by an unbalanced force changes speed and direction.

An object at rest stays at rest.

An object acted upon by a balanced force stays at rest.

An object acted upon by an unbalanced force changes speed and direction.

Newton's Second Law of Motion

The second law of motion describes the action of a force on a massive body, such as a planet or a star. It states: The relationship between an object's mass, its acceleration and the force applied to it is given by the formula, F = mass x acceleration. When a constant force acts on a planet, it continues to accelerate at a constant rate in the direction of the force.

Newton's second law concerns those objects upon which unequal forces act. An object on which all forces are balanced is said to be at equilibrium and such an object will not accelerate. Only an object with net force acting on it is capable of acceleration, and an increase in the force will also increase its acceleration.

Newton's Third Law of Motion

Among the three laws of motion, the most well-known is the third law of motion which states that: Every action has an equal and opposite reaction.

When a rocket ignites the fuel underneath it, the expanding exhaust gas pushes the rocket upwards. The effect is less noticeable in the case of a massive body. For instance, if you throw a ball while standing on the ground, you will cause the Earth's rotation to speed up by a negligible amount that can be safely ignored. On the other hand, if you throw a ball while standing on a skateboard, you'll move backwards by a noticeable amount.

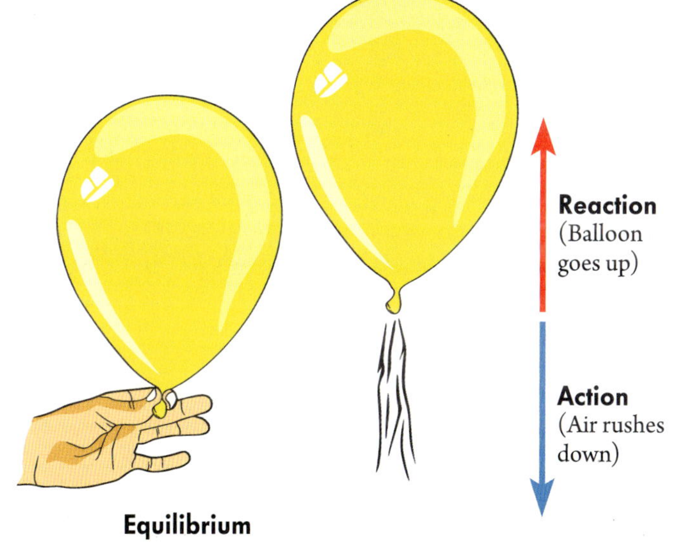

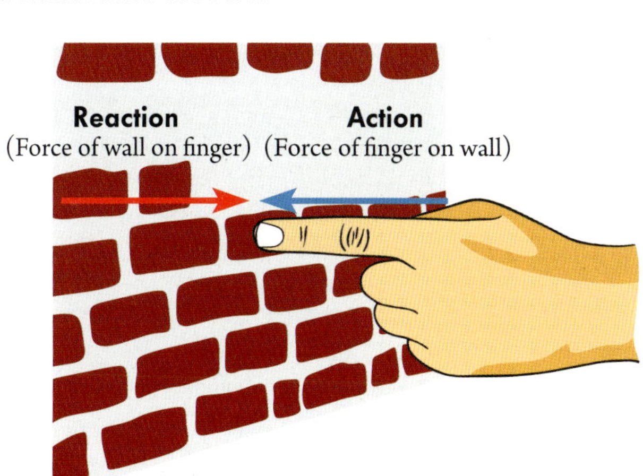

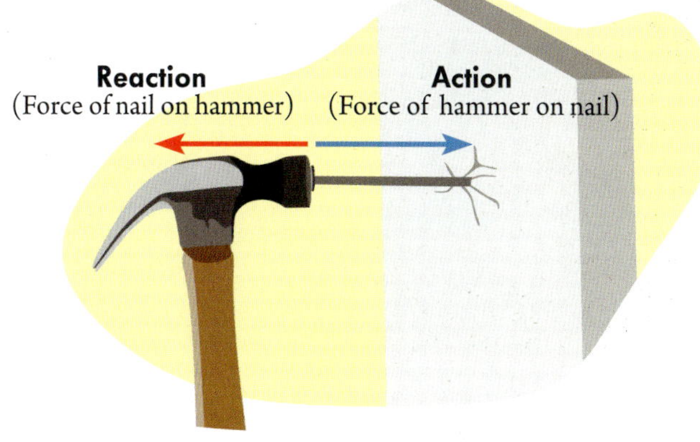

MOMENTUM

Any object that is in motion possesses momentum. In simple terms, momentum refers to the force or impetus gained by a moving object. Momentum of objects can give rise to collision. Moving objects in the same path tend to hit or collide with each other. An explosion is an event that propels objects into motion.

What is Momentum?

The momentum of an object is a product of its mass and velocity. So, going by the equation, a lightweight object or an object moving slowly will have a lower momentum. Consider a bowling pin versus a ping pong ball hurled at pins. The bowling pin, due its mass, gains more momentum and is more likely to knock out the pins than the ping pong ball.

Most objects in the universe possess momentum, that is, they continue moving in a specific direction unless they encounter an obstacle that makes them change direction.

A bowling ball striking pins is an example of collision.

Billiard balls traveling around the table encounter elastic collision.

Collision and its Types

Collision occurs when two objects strike against each other. When objects collide, they experience force briefly. This force changes the momentum of the objects. There are two types of collision:

Elastic collision: Any collision involving objects that get separated after colliding is elastic collision. The kinetic energy is conserved in this type of collision. The balls traveling on a billiards table are an example of elastic collision.

Inelastic collision: This is a type of collision between two bodies that result in a loss of energy. Even though the momentum is conserved, the kinetic energy is lost. Most collisions occurring in nature are inelastic. A bullet piercing wood is an example of an inelastic collision.

Law of Momentum Conservation

The law of momentum conservation states that if two objects collide in an isolated system, the total momentum before collision is equal to the total momentum after collision. The momentum lost by one object is transferred to the other object.

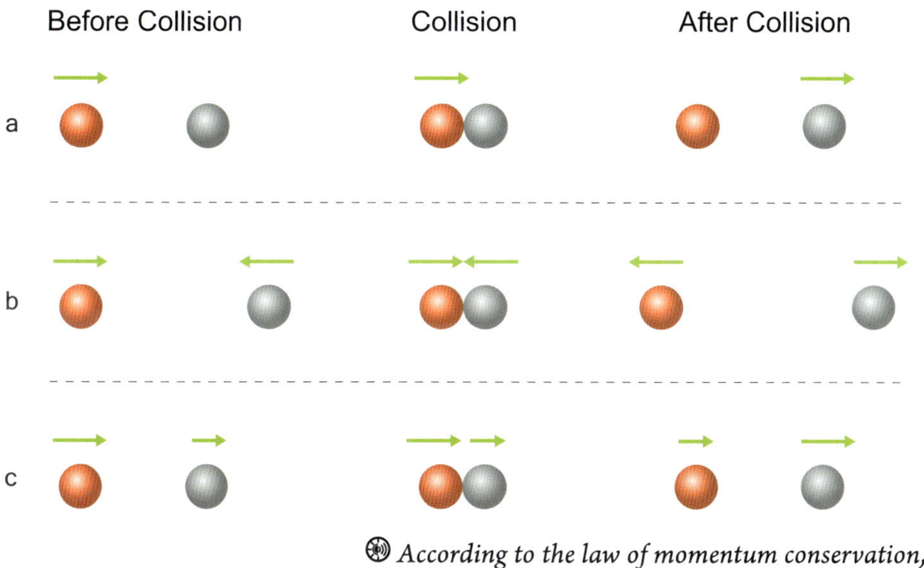

A bullet piercing partially through wood is a type of inelastic collision.

According to the law of momentum conservation, momentum before and after collision are equal.

When the net force acting on an object is zero, the momentum is said to be constant. In an elastic collision, as in the case of a ball striking the ground and bouncing back, no kinetic energy is lost. The energy and momentum is still conserved in the object. In an inelastic collision, as in the case of dropping a piece of clay, the kinetic energy is not lost. As it slams into the ground, the energy is converted into heat, sound or light.

Explosion

An explosion is an event that results in the propulsion of parts of an object in different directions as a result of an internal impulse. For instance when a bomb explodes, shards that are sent flying possess momentum. If the total momentum of the individual shards were measured, it would be equal to the total momentum. During an explosion, just as in a collision, the total momentum before and after the event is maintained.

An explosion results in the momentum of shards.

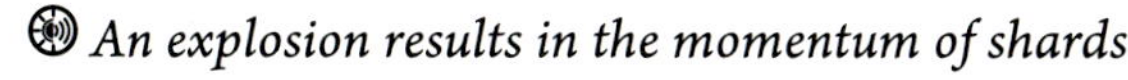

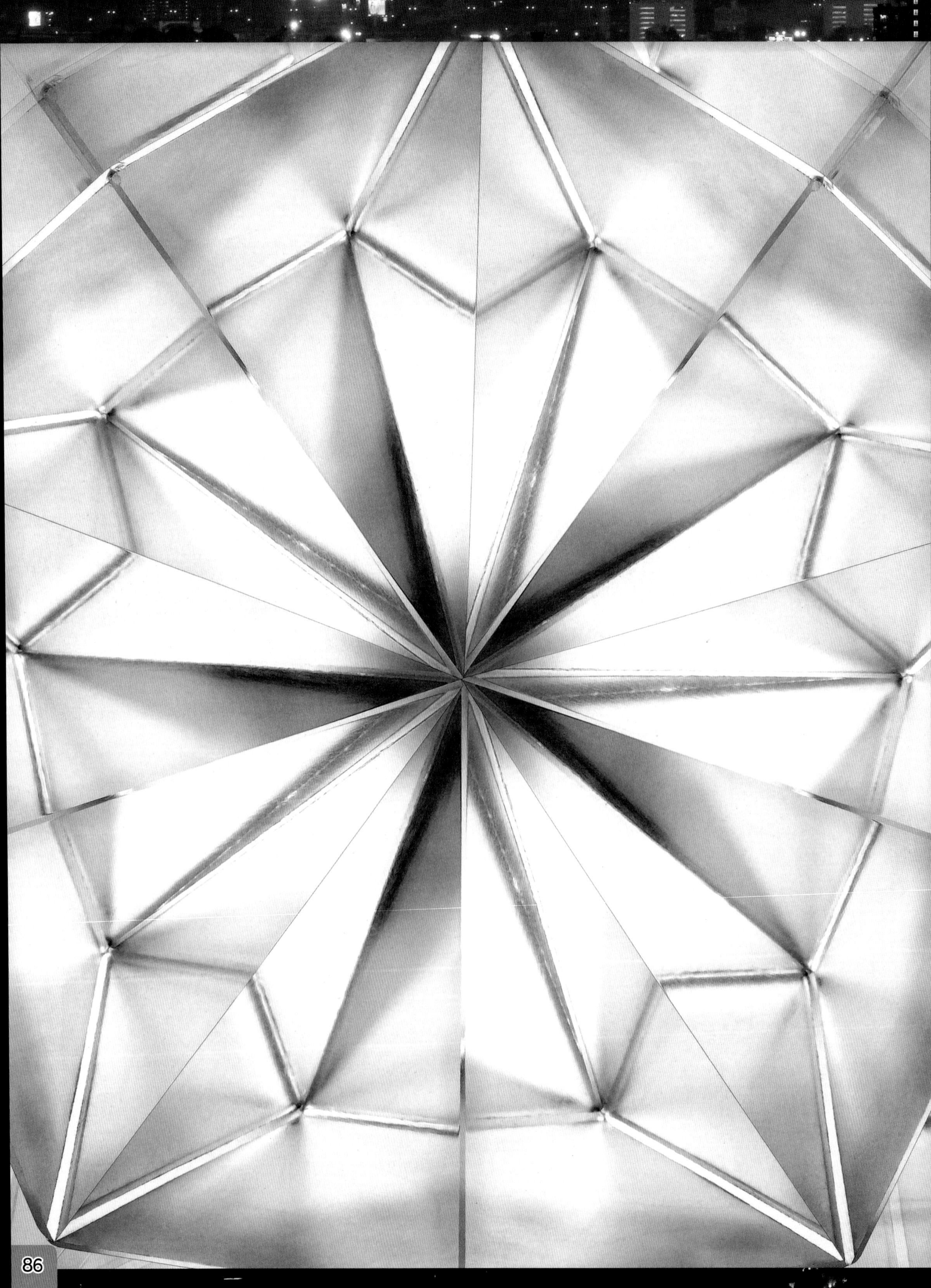

A First Introduction to Science

ENCYCLOPEDIA of LEARNING

DISCOVER
ELECTRICITY
& MAGNETISM

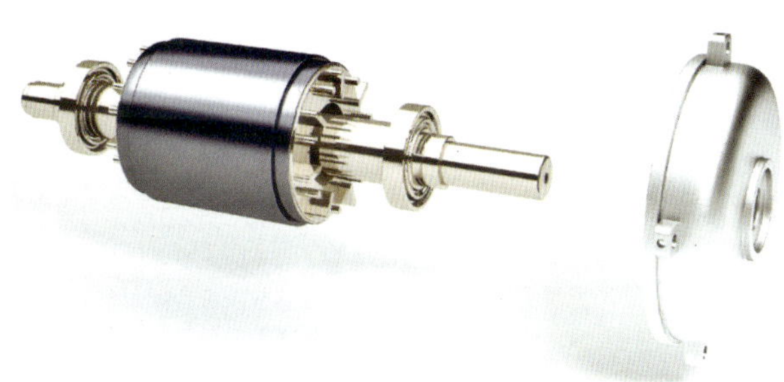

Introduction to Electricity

Electricity is associated with stationary or flowing electrons. The word 'electricity' is derived from the Greek word 'elektron' which means 'amber'. We use electricity to power household objects and also to run massive factories and organisations. Electricity is generated from different sources to meet the demands of houses, public resources and industries.

Nature of Electricity

Everything around us is made up of atoms. The atom has a nucleus with protons and neutrons, and electrons revolve around the nucleus. The nucleus has a net positive charge (protons are positively charged and neutrons do not have any charge). The electrons are negatively charged. The electrons and the nucleus attract each other due to opposite charges.

Electrons are capable of moving from one atom to another in a material that is capable of conducting electricity. Normally, the electrons move randomly and irregularly across the atoms in every direction, so there is no net movement of charge and no flow of electrons. When free electrons move or flow in one direction, it creates an electric current.

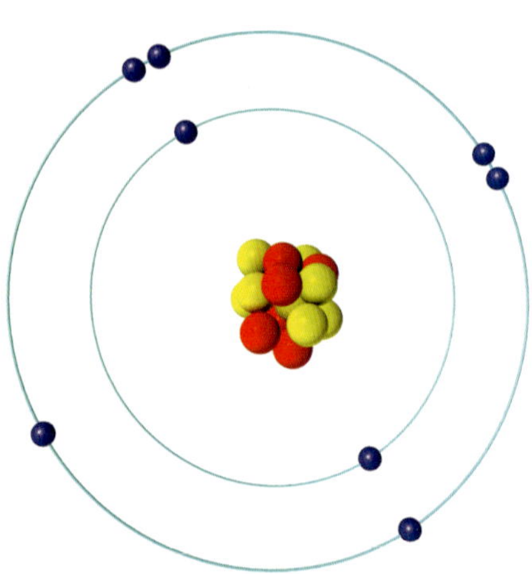

▼ Atom

▼ Lightning

Understanding Electricity: A Brief History

Much before people understood electricity, they observed and marveled at the power of lightning and how it sometimes struck down on someone or something. The ancient people of different civilisations were also aware of species of fish and sting rays that were capable of inducing electric shocks.

In 600 BC, Thales of Miletus, a Greek philosopher, discovered the phenomenon of static electricity when he rubbed fur and amber and used the amber to pick up small scraps and dust.

William Gilbert, who discovered the science of magnetism, was also responsible for using the term 'electricus' that later gave rise to the term 'electricity'. Later, in the 18th century, Benjamin Franklin conducted experiments in electricity, the most famous among them being the one in which he used a kite and a key during a lightning storm to prove that lightning was electrical in nature.

Many others played an important role in understanding electricity and enabling its use. Alessandro Volta invented the electrical battery. Michael Faraday studied electricity extensively and also developed the electric motor. Thomas Edison and Nikola Tesla also made important contributions in the field of electricity. While Edison is credited for the invention of the light bulb, Tesla invented the alternating current (AC) system that is used extensively today.

▲ Benjamin Franklin

▲ Michael Faraday

Types of Electricity

Static electricity and current electricity are the two types.

Static electricity: It is caused by the buildup of electric charges (positive or negative) on the surface of certain materials. This kind of electricity is produced due to friction or contact. The effects of static electricity are observed as sparks, shocks, or clinging of materials.

Current electricity: It is a form of electricity produced when electrons flow in one direction inside a conducting material.

▲ Electric lines

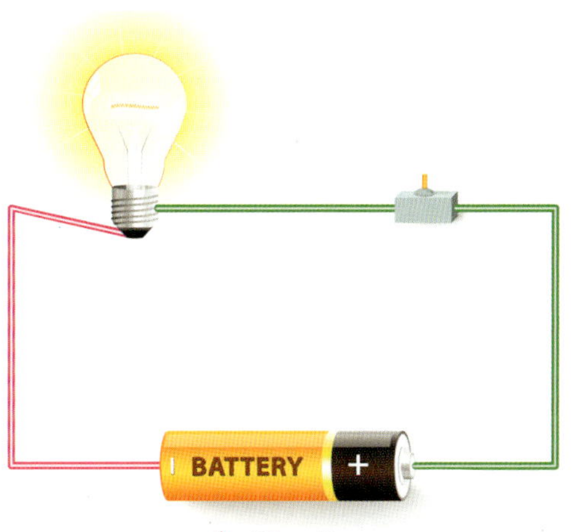

▲ Circuit

When the switch is flipped on, the electrons in the wire flow at nearly the speed of light, which is 3×10^8 metres/second!

Static Electricity

Static electricity is produced due to the buildup of electric charges on the surface of certain materials. When the materials are rubbed together or pulled apart, one material acquires a positive charge and the other acquires a negative charge, and the resulting imbalance produces static electricity in observable forms.

Static Electricity

Static electricity is so named to differentiate it from current electricity, where electrons flow. Two materials are involved in the generation of static electricity. One of these materials has an excess of electrons, or a negative charge. Another material that has lost electrons gains a positive charge. When these two materials interact by rubbing together, electrons are pulled from the surface of one material onto another. This effect is known as 'triboelectric charging.'

Static Electricity in Nature

In nature, static electricity is formed under different conditions. Usually, low humidity and dry air is ideal for generation of static electricity. When the air is humid or carries a lot of water vapour, the water molecules can collect on the materials and prevent the buildup of electrical charges.

However, extreme turbulence in the air caused by a thunderstorm cloud can result in static charge generation as the water drops down from the clouds. Benjamin Franklin performed a dangerous experiment by flying a kite with a metal key string attached to it during a storm. The static electricity caused an electric spark in the key.

◄ Hair standing up due to static electricity

Effects of Static Electricity

Static electricity causes any of the following effects:

Attraction: When a balloon is vigorously rubbed on a wool sweater, the balloon acquires a negative charge on its surface while the wool acquires a positive charge. The balloon can then be made to stick temporarily to the wall, which does not have an excess of either positive or negative charge. The same effect is observed when you comb your hair and use the comb to attract small shreds of paper.

▲ Balloon and paper attraction

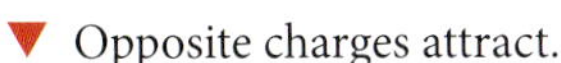
▼ Opposite charges attract.

Repulsion: When you use a plastic comb on dry hair, the comb acquires negative charges in the process. The strands of hair, left with an excess of positive charges, will repel each other resulting in them sticking up for a few seconds.

Sparks: Sparks are produced under circumstances when there are enough positive charges on one material and negative charges on another material. In such a case, the attraction between the positive and negative charges is so great that it makes electrons jump the air gap between the two objects. Such jumping electrons heat up the air and this, in turn, causes more electrons to jump across the gap. When the air gets hot enough, it glows briefly, resulting in a spark.

Lightning is an example of a powerful form of static electricity. The temperature of a lightning bolt can reach 28,000°C.

▲ Static electricity causing sparks

Static Electricity

▲ Electroscope

There are many methods to artificially produce static electricity by using suitable materials. Static electricity can also be generated in specially designed devices for research and demonstration. Static electricity can be harnessed and employed for different purposes.

Static Electricity Devices

Electroscope: This is one of the first known electrical measuring instruments. It was invented by William Gilbert around 1600. The electroscope is used for roughly measuring the presence and magnitude of electric charge. The device detects the electric charge of an object through its movement. However, this device is only useful for measuring more than hundreds of thousands of volts.

Electrophorus: This device was invented by a Swedish scientist, Johan Carl Wilcke, in 1764 and later its design was improved by Alessandro Volta. It combines the creation of static electricity along with electrostatic induction to charge a metal plate repeatedly. Static electricity charges are induced on the plate by rubbing with wool or fur. The plate develops negative charge. When a metal plate is then brought into contact, the two plates attract. When the plates are pulled apart, the charges are transferred onto the metal plate and can be used for producing sparks for demonstrating static electricity.

▲ Electrophorus

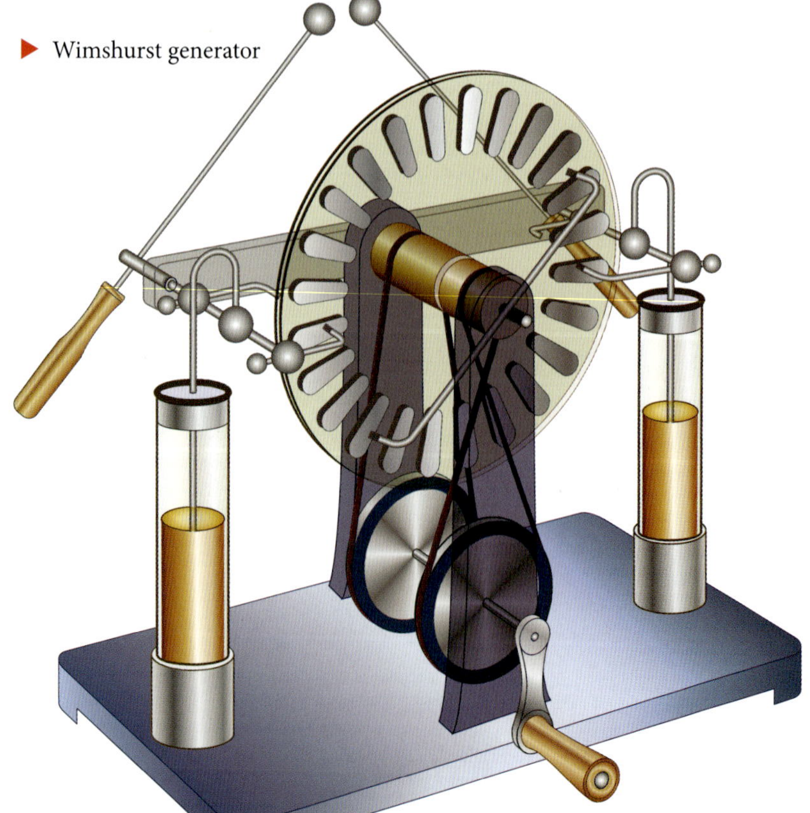

▶ Wimshurst generator

Wimshurst generator: Modern versions of Wimshurst generators—originally invented in the 1880s—consist of two plastic discs that rotate in opposite directions through a crank or belt-driven mechanism. As the discs turn, the metal foil sectors get charged and the accumulated charges are transmitted to a storage capacitor. This generator can produce up to 75,000 volts. Despite the high voltage, the current is low enough so that it isn't dangerous. This generator is used for producing sparks and conducting static electricity experiments.

Van de Graaff generator: This generator is powered by a high-speed electric motor and consists of two pulleys and a belt running along it. The lower pulley is an insulating material, while the upper pulley is made of metal. The high speed of the belt movement and buildup of a massive amount of charge enables it to produce great voltages of about 400,000 volts. Large generators can produce sparks that can travel across a room.

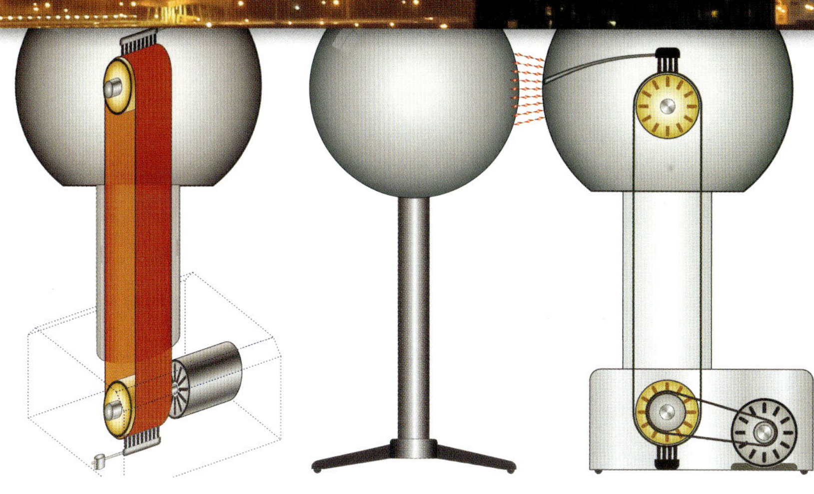

▲ Van de Graaff generator

Uses of Static Electricity

It might be easy to assume that static electricity is mostly useful only for the purpose of studying and demonstration. But static electricity has a few other practical uses too:

Painting cars: Automobile manufacturers employ static electricity for painting cars. The car's surface is first prepared for painting and placed in a painting booth. Specially designed, electrically charged paint is sprayed as a fine mist into the booth. The charged particles get attracted to the car's surface and stick to the body evenly and are distributed smoothly after drying, which cannot be achieved by manual painting.

Photocopying documents: A standard photocopier machine works on the principle of static electricity to make copies of documents. Electrically charged ink is used for specifically sticking to certain places on the paper.

Pollution control: Devices that can collect charged dirt particles in the air onto a plate with opposite charge are used for clearing a space of dirt and dust. This type of device is known as an electrostatic precipitator.

Smokestack: In factories that produce smoke, static electricity is used to reduce air pollution. The smoke is electrically charged so that it clings to electrodes of the opposite charge, which are placed in the smokestacks instead of being released into the air.

Air fresheners: Air fresheners work on a principle similar to the pollution control in smokestacks. The devices are capable of removing electrons from smoke, dust, and pollen, and the positively charged particles are then attracted to a negatively charged plate in the air freshener, resulting in cleaner air.

The Van de Graaff generator, despite producing high voltages, generates only enough electric current needed to light up a 4-watt bulb.

◀ Photocopier

Current Electricity

The movement of electrical energy from one place to another so that it can be utilized for powering devices is called current electricity. An electric current is produced by the motion of electrons in a suitable conducting material.

▲ Electric wires

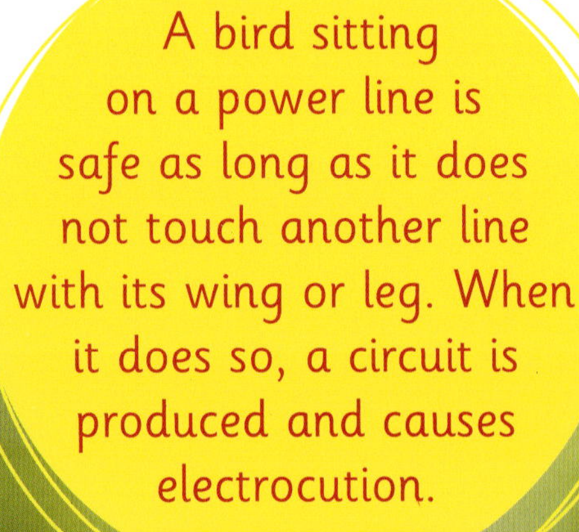

A bird sitting on a power line is safe as long as it does not touch another line with its wing or leg. When it does so, a circuit is produced and causes electrocution.

Electric Current and Voltage

The movement of charged particles (electrons), from one section to another, produces an electric current. The electrons are in motion along a specific path, which may be a conducting material like copper, aluminium or silver.

The electric current depends on the rate at which the electric charge flows through the conductor. A pump can be used to force water to flow quicker through a pipe. Similarly, using an external source of power such as a battery can push free electrons faster through the conductor in a specific path. If more electrons pass a given point in a second, the current is said to be greater. Current is measured in amperes.

Voltage is a measure of the difference in electrical energy between two points in an electric circuit. It is measured in volts.

◄ Bird on a power line

Resistance

Any force that opposes the motion of the electrons in a conducting wire is known as resistance. If a thin wire is used, the electrons do not have enough space to flow smoothly, and in this case the wire is said to have high resistance. In contrast, a thick wire provides more space for the movement of electrons and has lower resistance. Resistance is measured in ohms.

In simple terms, resistance refers to any obstruction in the way of electricity. If you think of an electric circuit with a light bulb in between, the bulb is a source of resistance. The obstacle uses up some of the electricity flowing through the circuit.

Uses of Current Electricity

Electrical devices: Morse code and the telegraph were invented using long-distance transmission through electricity.

Light sources: The first use of electricity for homes was for lighting. Light bulbs were followed by better and improved lights and lamps.

Batteries: Batteries are capable of converting chemical energy into electrical energy and are used for powering video games, remote-controlled toys, flashlights, and other small devices.

▲ Electric bulb

▲ Motor

Motors: Motors are used for powering many appliances including power tools, water pumps, vehicles, and industrial machines. A motor converts electrical energy into mechanical energy.

Medical uses: Many machines used in diagnosis and treatment of patients require electricity. A few examples of medical diagnosis devices include electrocardiograms, X-ray machines, scanning devices and ventilation systems.

Generators: All modern establishments like hospitals, schools, colleges, workplaces, factories, and shops use generators as backup when the power supply fails. A battery can store electrical energy for later use.

▶ Electric generator

Conductors and Insulators

Materials are classified as conductors or insulators based on their ability to conduct electricity. Both conductors and insulators are useful, and often both are used together, as in the case of wires for combining utility and safety.

Conductors

Conductors are those materials that permit electrons to move freely from atom to atom. A conducting material will allow electric charge to distribute across its entire surface, when charge is transferred to a certain location. The distribution of charge happens due to movement of electrons. When the conductor is touched by another conductor, the charge can be transferred through the free movement of electrons. Materials that are capable of high conductivity are referred to as superconductors.

Examples of conductors include metals such as iron, silver, aluminium, and copper; their alloys such as brass and bronze; ionic salts dissolved in water; graphite; and the human body.

▲ Conducting materials

The Van de Graaff generator is useful for proving that the human body is conductive to electric charge. When a person touches the static ball of the generator, the excessive charge on the ball is transferred to the person and spreads everywhere, including the hair. When all the hair strands acquire the same charge, they repel each other and stand straight up.

Charge Distribution

It is possible to predict the direction in which the electrons move in a conducting material by applying two rules of charge interaction: 1) Opposite charges attract; 2) Like charges repel.

If a conductor imparts a net negative charge at one location, there is an excess of electrons in that spot. Since the electrons all possess the same negative charge, they repel each other and try to move away or distance themselves. These electrons then begin to migrate on the conductor, distributing evenly across the surface.

When the conductor is instead given a positive charge by removing electrons, there is an excess of protons instead, but the same two rules of charge interaction apply. Since protons are bound to the nucleus and are not capable of movement, the electrons will help distribute the charge evenly across the surface. Electrons that are loosely bound to their atoms leave and move over to other atoms. The electron migration continues until the overall repulsion effect is minimized.

Insulators

Insulators are materials that impede the free flow of electrons between atoms. If electric charge is transferred to an insulator, the excess charge will remain in the location of transfer and will not be distributed across its surface ,as free movement of electrons does not occur. Rubber, plastic, ceramic, glass, Styrofoam, paper and dry air are examples of insulators.

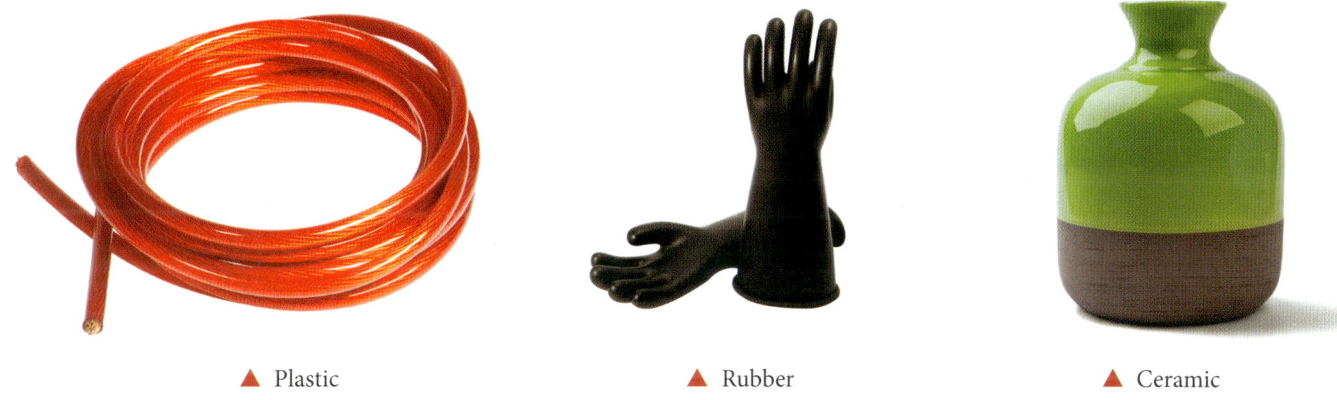

▲ Plastic   ▲ Rubber   ▲ Ceramic

Increasing Conducting Ability

Insulators			Semiconductors					Conductors				
Rubber	Glass	Wood	Dry air	Silicon	Germanium	Water	Mercury	Carbon	Iron	Aluminium	Copper	Silver

Uses of Conductors and Insulators

Conductors are used for transferring electric charge in the form of objects and wires. Owing to their conducting nature, conductors are mounted on top of or surrounded by an insulator material for safety. Household appliances have copper wires enclosed in plastic or rubber coating to avoid electric shock. Experiments are often performed using conductors mounted on insulators to enable them to be manipulated safely.

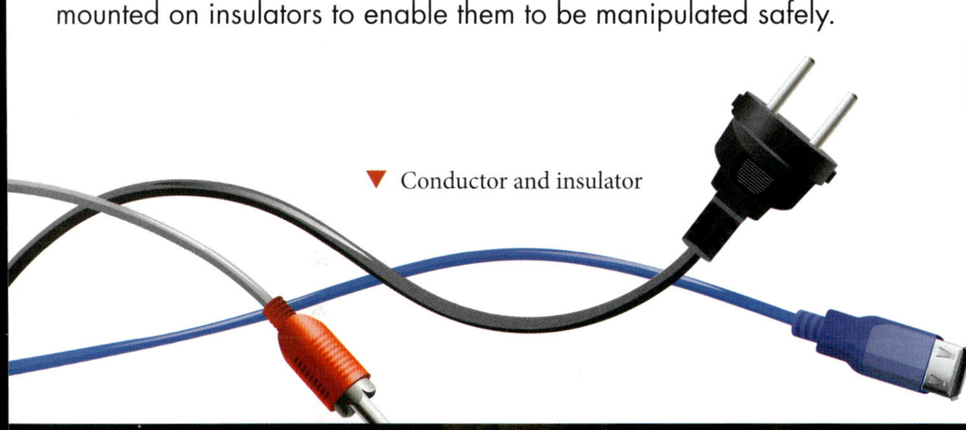

▼ Conductor and insulator

A metal conductor may be up to 10^{18} (a million trillion) times more conductive than glass!

Electric Field

An electric field is an area that can influence charge within a circuit as the charge travels from one location to another. The electric force, like gravity, is a noncontact force that can influence without having to be directly in contact.

Electric Charge

Only charged particles exhibit an electric field. If the electrically charged particles are also moving, they generate a magnetic field. The combined electric and magnetic field is referred to as the electromagnetic field. Electric charge is the physical property of any particle to experience a force when placed in an electromagnetic field.

The electric charge can be either positive or negative. Any material which has no net charge is called neutral. Substances that have more protons than electrons have a positive charge, while those with more electrons than protons possess a negative charge.

Any object's total electric charge is calculated as the sum of the electrical charges of all the particles that make up the object. Usually, electric charge is small and insignificant because objects are made up of atoms that usually have the same number of electrons (negative charge) and protons (positive charge).

Electric Field

A single electric charge will attract or repel another charge brought close to it. This ability to attract or repel is stored in a certain region around the electric charge. This region is referred to as the electric field. All charged particles have electric fields around them.

A Van de Graaff generator is a good example of a charged object that generates an electric field. The field is so intense that without even having to touch the static ball, you can experience a strange sensation just as you pass by.

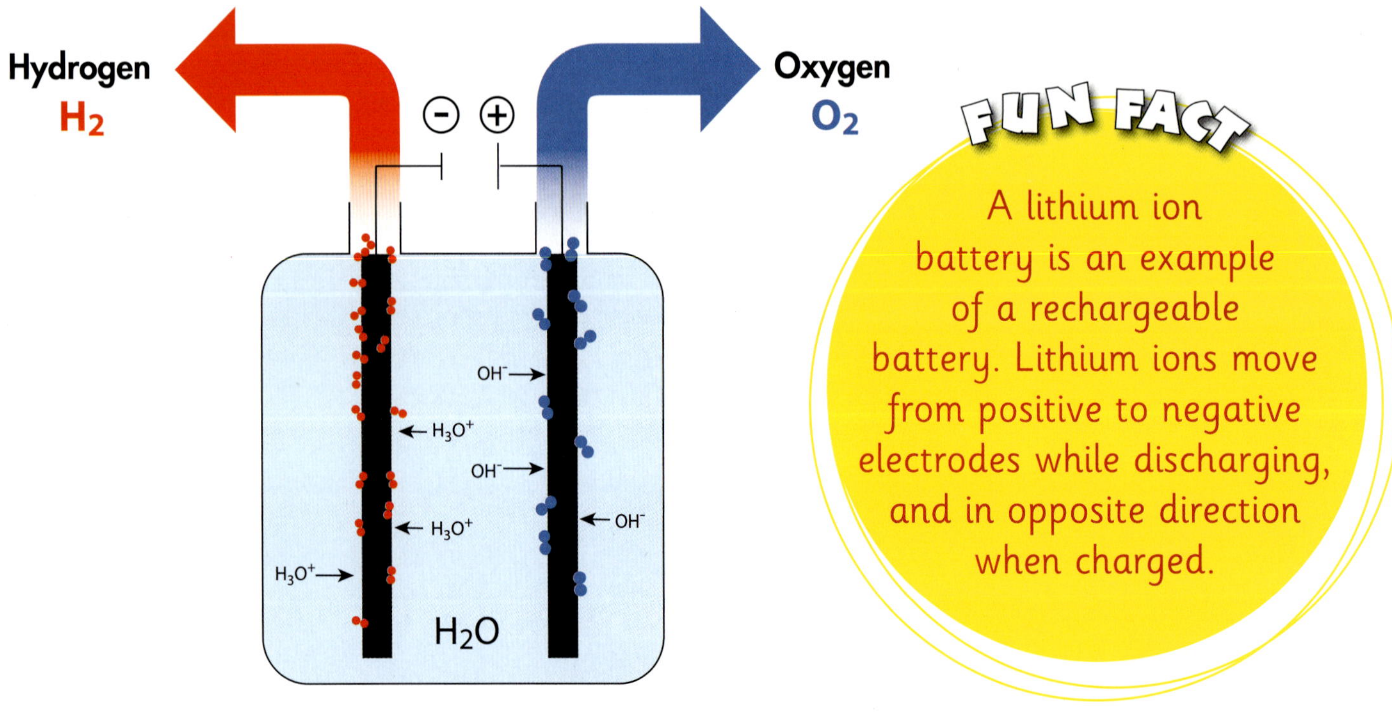

▲ Electric charge movement in solution

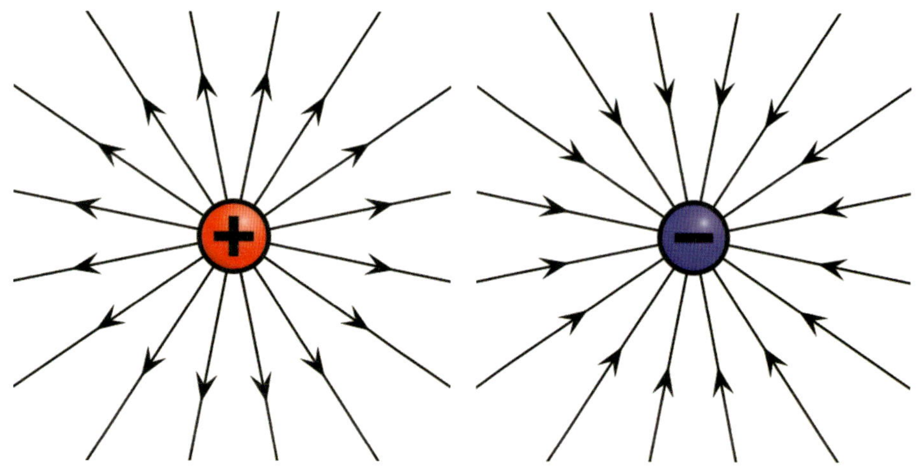

Lines of Force

An electric field can be visualized as imaginary lines known as the 'lines of force.' Even though the lines of force are imaginary, it is helpful for visualising the electric field. This field of force can exert its effect without direct physical contact. Any charged object when brought close to the electric field will alter the field in a certain way. The more a charged object moves into a field, the more pronounced and noticeable the effect.

▲ Lines of force

Electric lines of force can indicate the direction in which a positive or negative charge would move in the presence of another charge. The lines of force around a positively charged object radiate in all directions away from the object. The lines around a negatively charged object radiate toward the object.

When another object of opposite charge is brought close, the lines of force will connect. When similarly charged objects are brought close to each other, the lines of force will never connect. In order to move a charge in an electric field away from its natural direction, you must exert a specific external force.

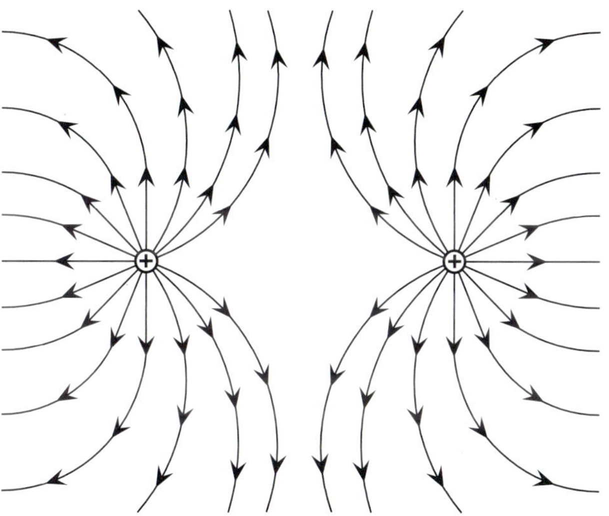

▲ Repulsion

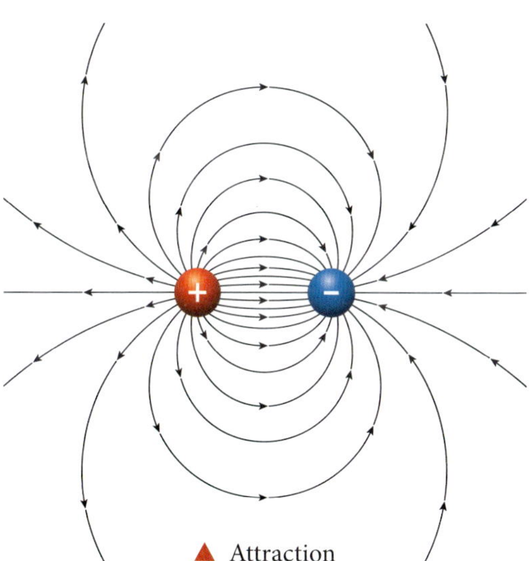

▲ Attraction

Nature of Electric Force

The electric force is the fundamental factor that keeps the electrons bound to the nucleus of an atom. It is this force that is responsible for chemical bonding between elements to produce molecules.

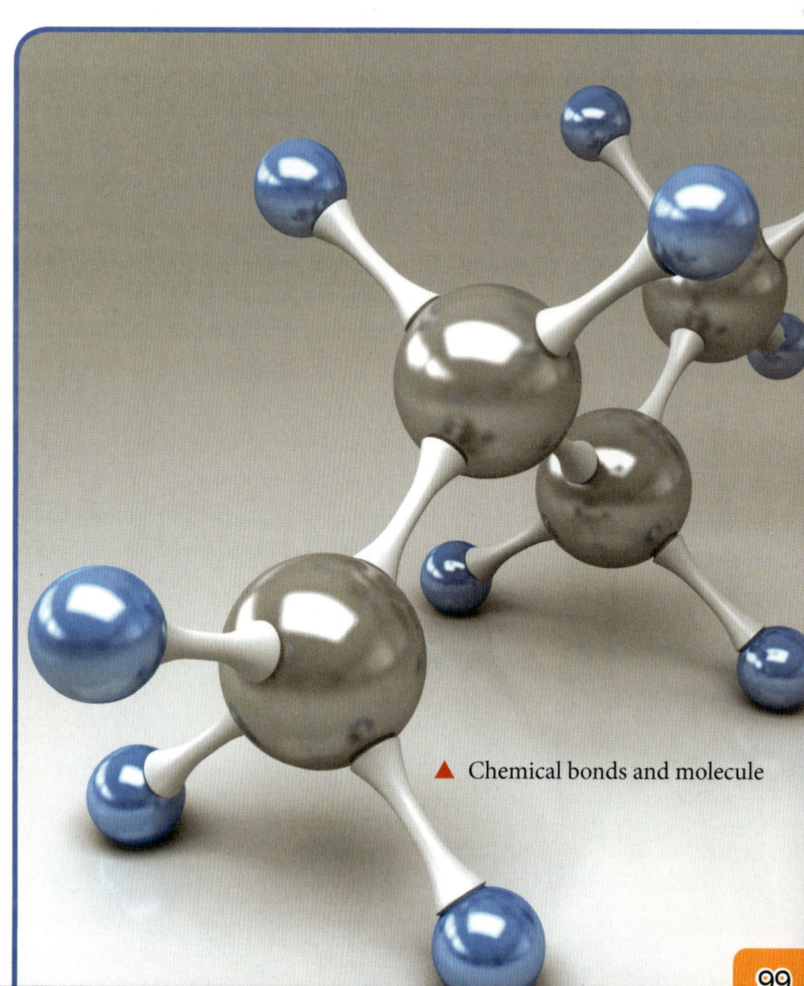

▲ Chemical bonds and molecule

Direct Current and Alternating Current

There are two main types of current: direct current DC) and alternating current (AC). They differ mainly in the direction in which the electric current flows. Both these types of current serve useful purposes depending on the need.

Direct Current

In Direct Current, the current flow is in a single direction and does not change periodically. Direct current is used for powering electrical devices and charging batteries. Fuel cells, solar cells, and batteries produce direct current. Electric vehicles, mobile phone batteries, flashlights, and flat-screen televisions use direct current. DC is represented as a straight line.

▶ Batteries

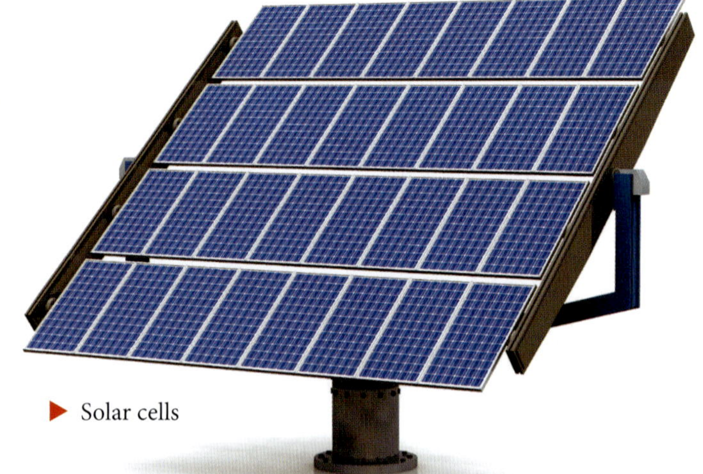

▶ Solar cells

In direct current, the electrons move slowly but continuously in one direction and travel from one end to the other. The voltage is also constant or almost constant. If you take a 1.5-volt battery, the voltage it provides will always be 1.5 volts. Similarly, the positive terminal will always remain the positive terminal, and the same holds true for the negative terminal. As a result, the electrons will move only in one direction.

Michael Faraday tested alternating current for the first time in 1832 using his dynamo electric generator.

Alternating Current

As the name suggests, alternating current (AC) keeps switching directions forward and backward periodically. It is the most commonly used type of current, and is preferred for powering household electrical appliances as well as for businesses. It is represented as a curved line wave form known as a sine wave. The waves or the curved lines represent the alternating current's cycles which are measured in hertz.

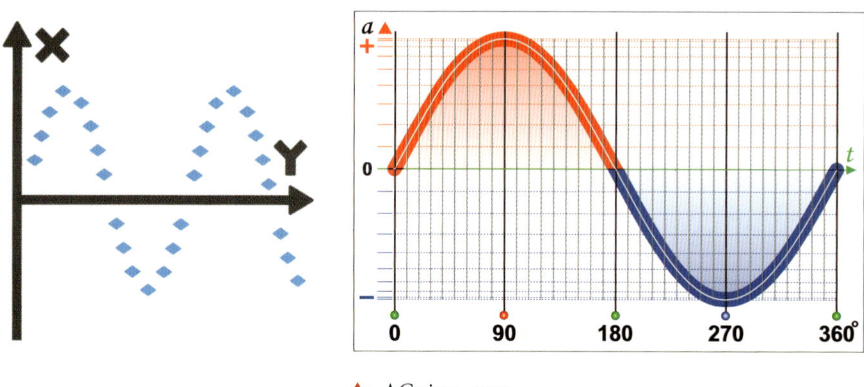

▲ AC sine wave

The voltage in alternating current periodically reverses itself, and every time this happens, the direction of the current flow changes. In power distribution systems across the world, the voltage is reversed about 50 to 60 times per second. The electrons do not move in a flow but instead wiggle back and forth—that is, they move in one direction, turn around, and move in the opposite direction so that the net effect is that they haven't moved.

The reason why alternating current is the preferred one for transmitting across long distances is its efficiency. Direct current loses more power than alternating current when it flows for long distances.

The mechanism of Newton's cradle explains how alternating current works. The device consists of a wooden frame with a series of metal balls hung in such a way that they are in a line and touching each other. If a ball at one end is pulled and released, it swings forward to propel the ball on the other end to swing, which in turn strikes back. The alternating motion can continue for a long time before the balls come to rest.

The electrons in AC move in one direction and then reverse and move in the opposite direction back and forth as long as the voltage reverses continuously. The voltage constantly changes from the maximum positive to zero and then to the maximum negative, then back to zero and so on in cycles.

In a power grid, a transformer is used for converting AC to high voltages (about 1 million volts) to make it easier to transmit across a long distance and then drop it back down to lower voltages for distribution to houses.

▼ Power station with grids

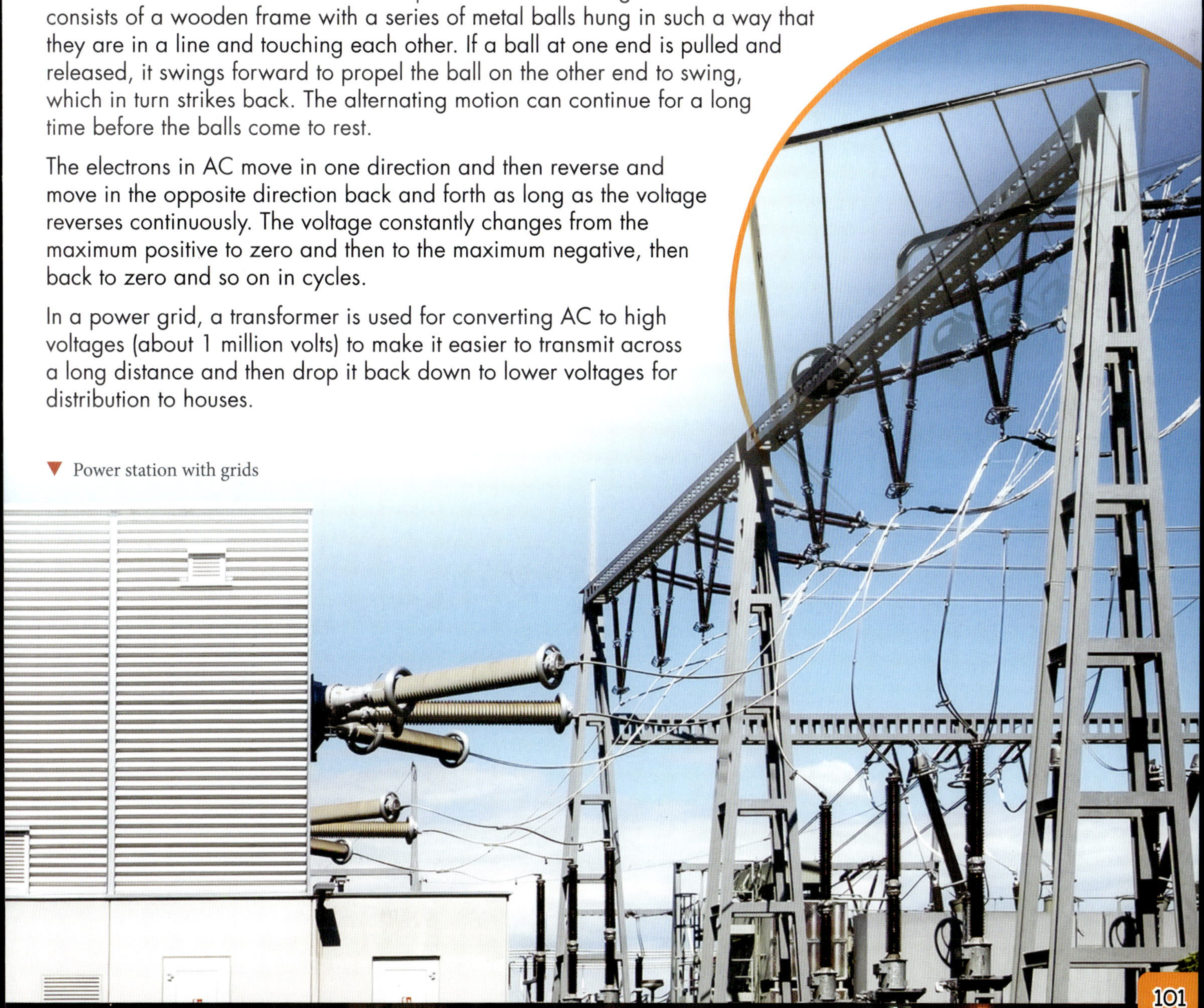

Electronics

Today, electronics are used everywhere, for functions ranging from storing money to guiding airplanes to monitoring your heartbeat. The science of electronics deals with manipulating electrons to control operations and process information. Electronics has enabled the development of computer technology and robotics.

▼ Electronic circuit

Difference between Electricity and Electronics

Electricity deals with making electrons flow around a circuit to drive a motor or an appliance. Generally, these electrical devices require a lot of energy to enable their function and deal with high levels of electric currents. Electronics, on the other hand, use tiny electric currents to power components. In theory, single electrons are carefully navigated around complex circuits to process signals. To give a comparison, if an electric kettle operates on a current of 10 amperes, an electronic component would use only a fraction of a milliampere.

Analog and Digital Signals

Electronic equipment can store data in analog or digital form. Radios used to be designed with antennae to catch radio waves transmitted from a radio station. The waves vibrate up and down in a pattern corresponding to the voices or music, and these signals are converted into sounds that can be heard. This is an example of analog signals. A modern radio works differently. The signals are received in the digital format as coded numbers and then converted into sounds.

Digital electronics dominate all types of modern electronic equipment such as smartphones, hearing aids, cameras, computers and tablets.

Electronic Circuits

An electronic device's function is decided not just by the components within it but also in the way those components are arranged in circuits. The simplest circuit is a continuous loop connecting two components, while a complicated circuit can have different circuit connections between more than two components.

▼ Electronic devices

Generally, analog appliances have simpler electronic circuits than digital appliances. For instance, a transistor radio will have a few components and a circuit board about the size of a book. On the other hand, a computer will have complex circuits with millions of separate pathways. A complex circuit can perform more intricate operations than a simple one.

Circuit Board

In the laboratory, a simple circuit can be assembled by connecting electronic components with the help of short lengths of copper cables. However, when one uses many components, it becomes difficult to connect them. To address this problem, components are arranged and assembled in a systematic way on a circuit board.

A circuit board is a rectangular piece of plastic with copper connecting tracks on one surface and holes drilled through it for connecting components by poking them through the holes and using the copper tracks to link them together or cutting off excess bits when necessary. Extra wires can also be added for making additional connections. This basic type of circuit board is also simply referred to as 'bread board.'

In electronic equipment, instead of these hand-assembled bread boards, factory-made plastic circuit boards with the circuit chemically printed on the surface are used. The copper tracks are also automatically created in a mass manufacturing facility. They are then pushed through pre-drilled holes and fastened into place. They are known as printed circuit boards (PCBs).

▲ Bread board

Microchips

It was the invention of microchips that created a revolution in the field of information technology. Miniature forms of electronic components were called integrated circuits. It is possible to squeeze millions of miniature components onto a chip no bigger than a person's fingernail. This also made it possible to make sleeker and faster computers and laptops.

▲ Microchip

Electronic Components

Electronic equipment is made up of many tiny components that perform different functions and are linked together through cables or metal connectors. These components are built from a small number of standard parts. These parts can be put together in different places to enable unique functions.

Despite their differences, electronic components have one factor in common. No matter what function they perform, the flow of electrons needs to be controlled in a very specific way. Also, all the solid components are made up of part-conducting and part-insulating materials. The combination of conducting and insulating materials in one component is also known as a semiconductor.

Some of the common electronic parts include:

Resistors: These are the simplest and most basic components of any electronic circuit. The main job of a resistor is to restrict the flow of electrons and thus control the flow of current flowing through the circuit. This is accomplished by converting electrical energy into heat. Resistors are available in different sizes.

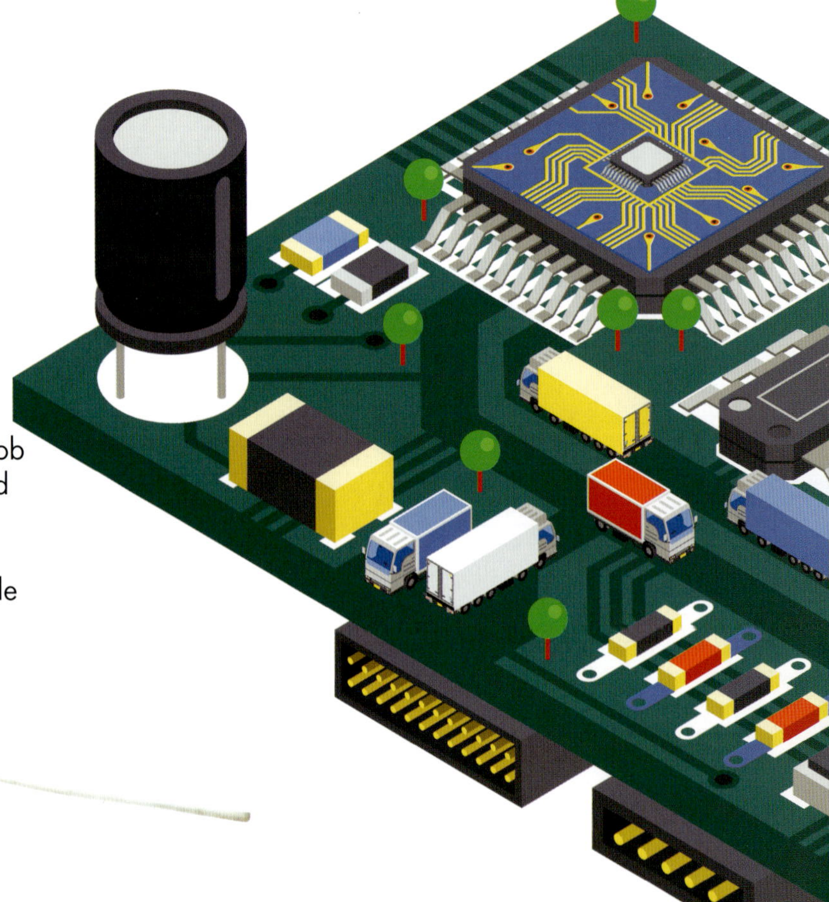

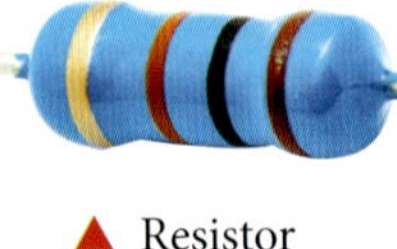

▲ Resistor

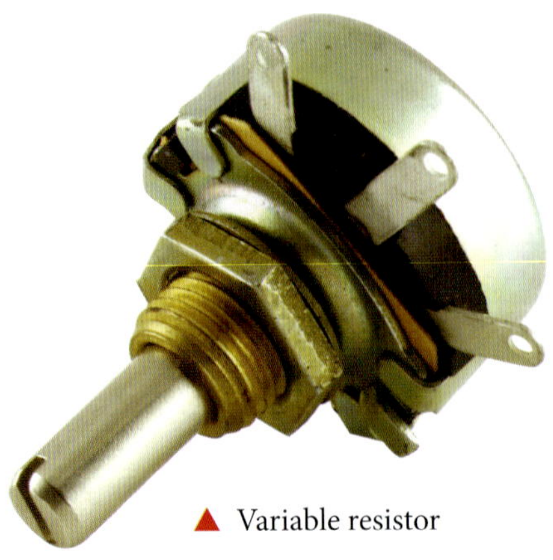

▲ Variable resistor

Capacitors: A capacitor is a simple component made up of two pieces of conducting material, usually made of metal, called 'plates' and separated by an insulating material called 'dielectric.' Capacitors can store electrical energy just like a battery. When a capacitor is recharged with energy, it is called 'charging' and when it releases energy it is said to be 'discharging.' The amount of electrical energy that a capacitor can store is known as 'capacitance.' They are most often used in timing devices. It is also useful as a tuning device in televisions and radios.

▶ Capacitor

Transistors: A transistor is a miniature electronic component made of silicon that can act as an amplifier or a switch. A transistor can take a small amount of electric current at one end and produce a much bigger output current through amplification. Hence, transistors are useful in hearing aids.

Since transistors can also function as switches, they are the major component of memory chips. Transistors that are connected together make devices that are called logic gates. These logic gates are useful in yes/no decision-making. A typical chip will have billions of transistors capable of being switched on or off.

▲ Transistor

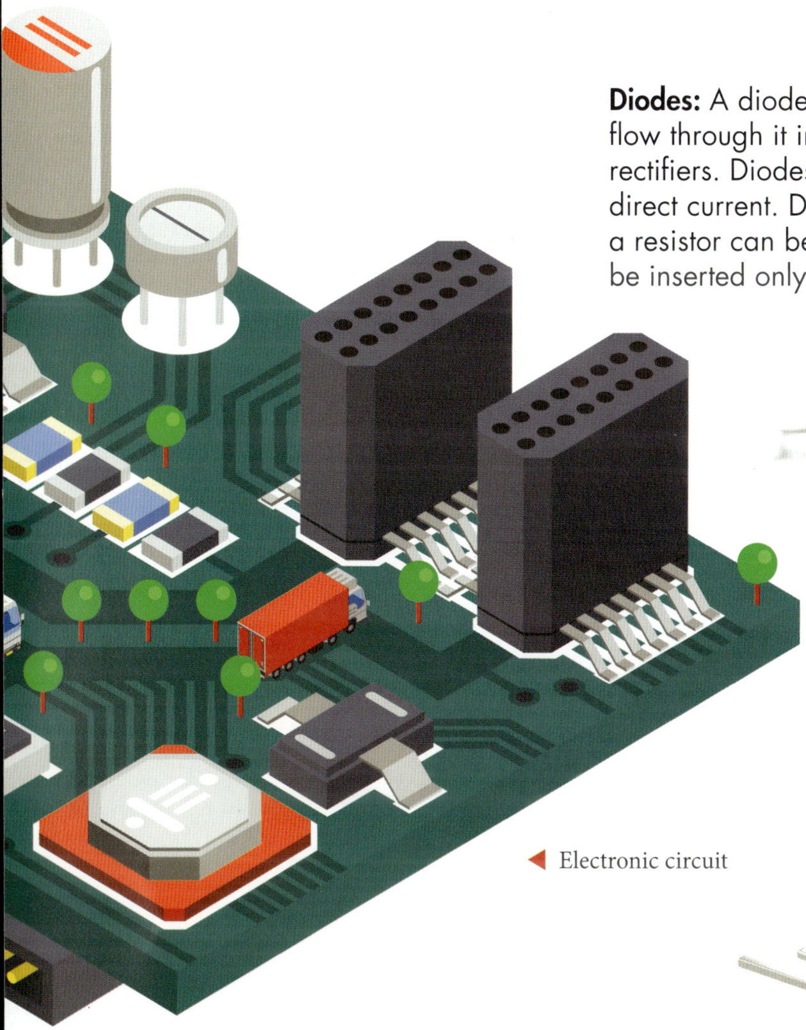

Diodes: A diode is an electronic component that allows current to flow through it in only one direction. Diodes are also known as rectifiers. Diodes are useful in converting alternating current to direct current. Diodes resemble a resistor but work differently. While a resistor can be inserted either way in a circuit board, a diode can be inserted only in a specific direction.

▲ Diode

Optical electronic components: A photoelectric cell is a type of electronic component that can produce tiny electric currents when light falls on it. In contrast, a light-emitting diode (LED) works in the opposite way by emitting light when it receives tiny electric currents.

◀ Electronic circuit

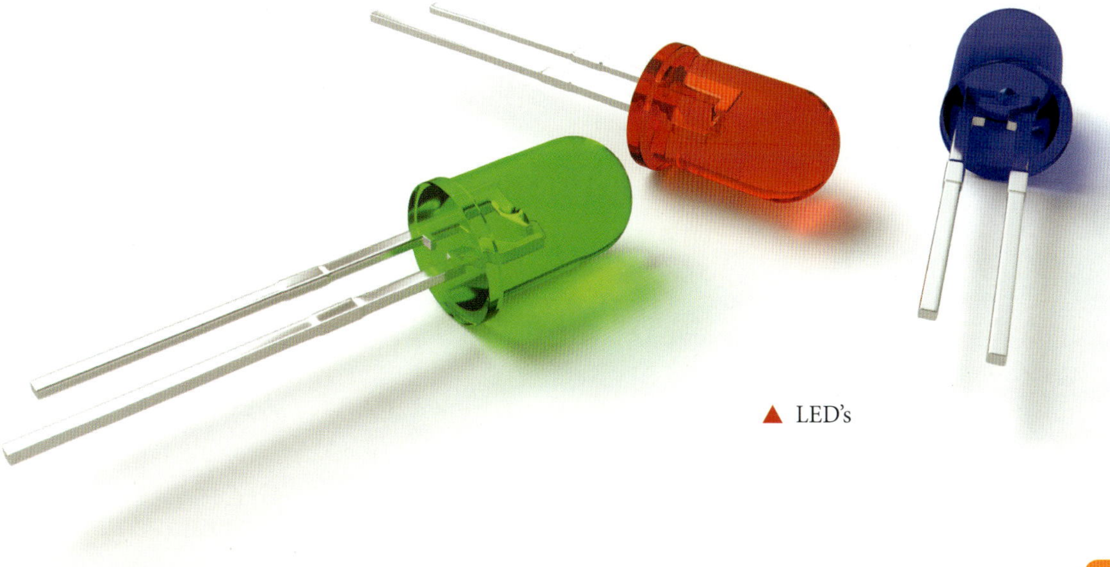

▲ LED's

Generation of Electricity

Electricity is necessary for the household, public, and industrial needs of people across the world. There are different ways to generate electricity, some of which are efficient or nonpolluting while others are inefficient or pollute the environment.

Electric Power Plants

Electric power plants use steam, water, wind, or gas combustion turbines to drive generators. An electricity generator is a device that converts the movement of magnetism inside a coil of wire into electric current. Generators operate on the basis of the relation between electricity and magnetism. The generator is equipped with insulated coils of wire and a rotating electromagnetic shaft. The combined currents produced in each coil add up to one large current that moves from the generator to the power lines and to the buildings.

Fossil Fuels

The dead and buried remains of plants and animals that lived millions of years ago gave rise to fossil fuels like coal, natural gas, and petroleum. Burning fossil fuels is a major source of electricity. However, burning fossil fuels can produce pollution and release of carbon dioxide. Fossils fuels are nonrenewable resources and will not last for long.

Fossil fuels

Thermal Power Plants

Thermal power plants use heat to generate electricity. Water is heated until it turns into steam of high temperature. When this steam is channeled through a turbine, it causes the blades in the shaft to spin, and when this rotor is connected to a generator, the movement is converted into electricity.

▼ Power station

FUN FACT

Currently, fossil fuels contribute to about 85 percent of the energy consumed across the world.

Nuclear Power

Nuclear plants and power stations generate electricity through steam generated from the heat produced by the atomic fission of radioactive elements like uranium and plutonium. Nuclear plants do not require massive amounts of fuel as in the case of fossil fuels. However, the many safety, health, and environmental hazards associated with the elements used make nuclear power controversial.

▲ Hydroelectric plant

Hydroelectric Plants

Hydroelectricity can be harvested from fast-moving currents in suitable water bodies or reservoirs with dams. Pumped storage is a type of hydroelectricity generated from water pumped through a turbine to generate electricity during periods of low water demand.

▲ Wind turbines

Geothermal Plants

Erupting geysers are a natural source of steam that can be used for generating electricity with very low levels of pollution. The thermal energy harvested from geothermal plants is used for electricity generation as well as heating purposes.

Wind Power

Wind power is generated from the motion of windmills and causes no pollution. However, wind energy is not as effective as water in generating electricity. The most effective way to harness wind power is to use a few large windmills or several small windmills. Only certain locations on the planet are suitable for generating wind power.

Fuel Cells

Fuel cells combine chemical substances to generate electricity through a continuous flow of fuel. Space shuttles are often powered by fuel cells that combine hydrogen and oxygen continuously to generate electricity and water. Fuel cells are not suitable for large installations providing mass power supply because they are difficult to make and operate.

Solar Power

Solar cells, also known as photovoltaic cells, consist of a series of cells wired together and capable of producing electricity when sunlight strikes them. Solar power is nonpolluting and the Sun is a continuous source of fuel. Even though not all the sunlight that strikes the panels is converted into electricity and they are expensive, solar power is still an attractive option for harnessing sunlight.

▼ Solar panels

Electrical Appliances

We use electricity every day to power all our appliances, and it comes from electrons moving in sync to produce heat, light, or movement. Electricity and magnetism work together as electromagnetism for making electrical appliances work.

▲ Fan

▲ Washing machine

All-purpose Motors

One thing common to all electrical appliances is that they are powered by electricity either in the form of batteries or direct plug-in power supplies through wall-mounted sockets. Apart from this, most of the appliances work by powering an electric motor. A motor is a device equipped with wire endings, magnets, and a rotating shaft.

The electrons in the wire begin to get organized and make the motor spin by turning the wire into an electromagnet. The magnets around the electromagnet are set up in such a way that the attractive and repulsive forces give rise to constant spinning motion in the electromagnet. When the motor receives electricity and converts it into rotational energy, this rotational energy can power a wide range of mechanical work.

Fans, washing machines, and other similar appliances work through the spinning motion of wheels or blades. This spinning motion is powered by motors that rotate when connected to a power supply. Food processors and blenders work in a similar way. They are powered by rotating blades attached to the motor's shaft.

Vacuum cleaners also use a motor to convert electrical energy to mechanical energy. In this appliance, the rotating device creates suction to pull in dirt and dust and will have an air intake, filter, and outlet.

▲ Vacuum cleaner

▲ Disassembled motor

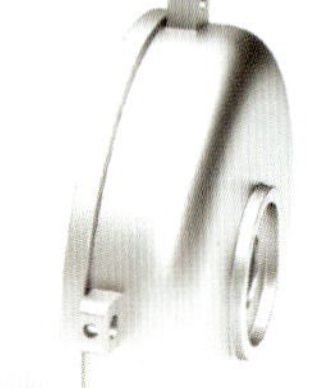

Heating Appliances

When current passes through wire, it naturally heats up a little. This is because of the movement of electrons as they bombard the metal atoms. The energy of the movement is given out as heat. Copper wires are generally used when there is a need for electrons to move around easily without expending too much energy as heat.

However, in appliances that need to produce heat, such as a blow dryer or toaster, wires are instead made of a nickel and chromium alloy called nichrome. When electrons pass through this alloy, they produce a lot of heat. At the atomic level, this is because the electrons often bump into nickel and chromium atoms (more frequently than in copper) and leak heat constantly.

▲ Toaster

▲ Generator

Generators

A generator is almost the reverse of an electric motor. A motor receives electricity as the input and provides rotational energy or mechanical energy as the output. A generator uses any other source to produce rotation, and electrical energy is the output. A gas-powered generator has a gasoline engine that can make a shaft turn, and this movement is converted into electricity.

A dynamo is a type of generator that converts the mechanical energy expended in pedaling into electricity to power the electric lamp. A small windmill is equipped with a generator that can convert the motion of the blades into electricity.

Safety

Since electric currents can be dangerous, appliances must be handled with care. Those that repeatedly blow a fuse must be repaired or replaced. Frays or cracks in electric cords must be replaced. No power outlet should be overloaded with too many appliances at the same time. Water and electricity should never mix—keep electric appliances away from water sources, and no switch or plug should be handled with wet hands.

▲ Safe handling of electrical appliances

Magnetism

Magnetism is a physical phenomenon exhibited by certain materials that make them capable of producing a magnetic field and attracting or repelling other similar substances.

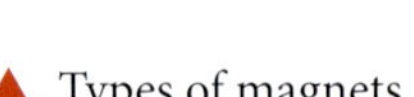

▲ Types of magnets

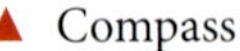

▲ Compass

▲ Magnetite (lodestone)

Understanding Magnetism: History

Magnetic materials were an ancient discovery. The ancient Greeks and Romans used what is known as lodestone, an iron-rich material, to attract other scraps of iron. The ancient Chinese even derived use from a magnet—they made magnetic compasses that they used for practicing a form of art, feng shui. These compasses were later used for navigation.

▶ Bar magnet

In the 13th century, Petrus Perigrinus, a French scholar, became one of the first people to study magnetism in detail and describe the properties of magnets. Afterward, William Gilbert, an English physician, analyzed the behaviour of magnets and was the first person to propose that the Earth behaved like a giant magnet. Over the next decades, more studies enabled a better understanding of what causes magnetism and its relation to electricity.

Properties of Magnets

Magnets always have two poles, a north pole (or a north-seeking pole) and a south pole (south-seeking pole).

The north pole attracts the south pole and repels the north pole of another magnet. In other words, like poles repel and unlike poles attract.

A magnet creates an invisible area of attraction or repulsion around it, which is known as its magnetic field.

The north pole of a magnet points towards the Earth's North Pole. This is because the Earth itself behaves like a giant magnet.

Cutting a magnet will not change its polarity of north and south poles. You'll merely get two magnets with their respective north and south poles.

Heating a magnet will make it lose some or all of its magnetic property.

Running a magnet over a magnetic material like an iron nail or a piece of nickel will convert that material into a magnet. This property is known as magnetisation.

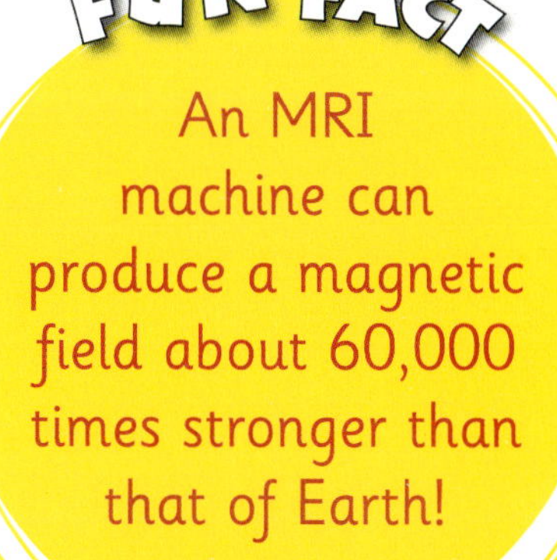

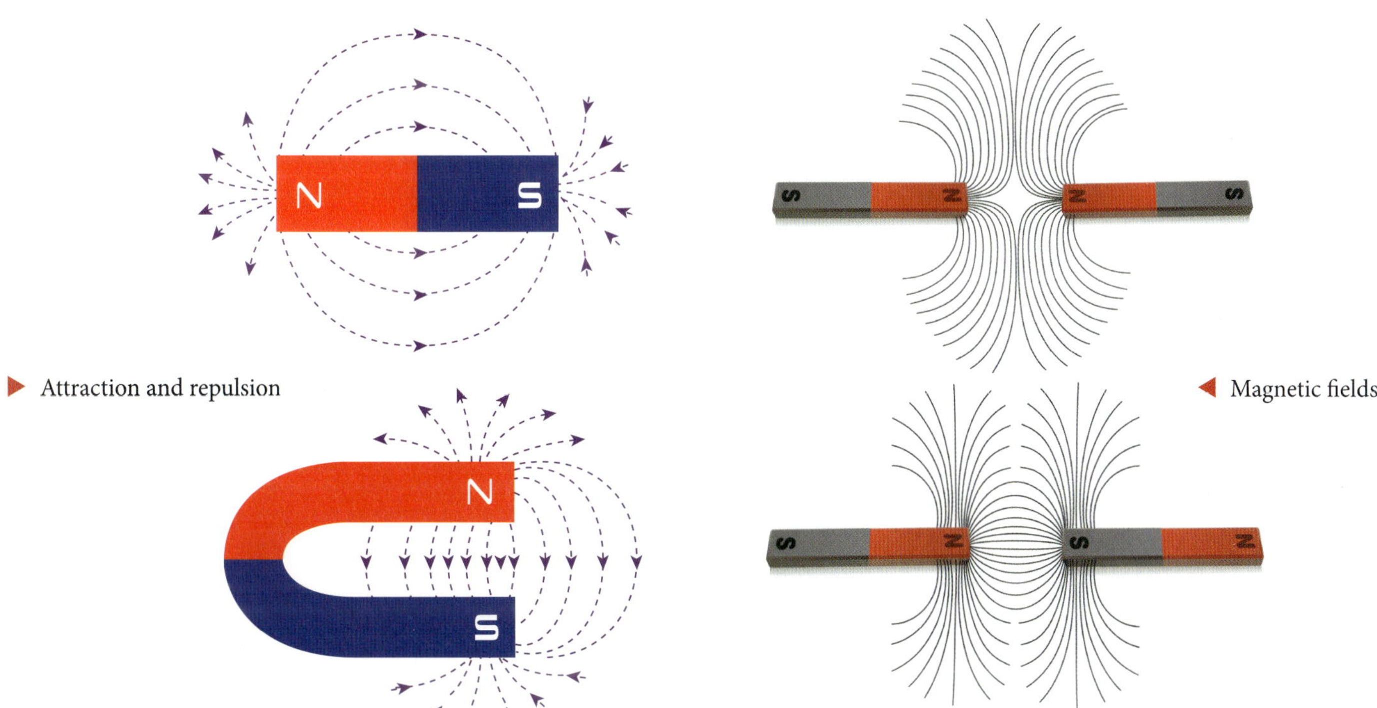

▶ Attraction and repulsion

◀ Magnetic fields

How Magnetism Works

Long before a detailed understanding of atoms and subatomic particles existed, the domain theory was used to explain magnetism. According to the theory, an iron bar (or any strong substance) contains many tiny pockets called domains. When the domains are arranged haphazardly, there is no magnetism. But when these domains are arranged in the same way, there is an overall magnetic field. When the iron bar is rubbed with a magnet, it becomes magnetized and all the domains that were originally haphazard are aligned so that they're pointing in the same way.

Later, it was discovered that the explanation for magnetism was inside the atoms that made up the magnetic material. More precisely, magnetism is the result of the rapid spinning of electrons. Since electrons are electrically charged particles, their motion resulted in magnetism. Each electron produced a tiny magnetic field. The sum total of the all these magnetic fields in a magnetic substance gives it its magnetic property.

Magnetic Field

The region surrounding a magnetic material or a moving electrical charge that can attract or repel other magnets or electric charges nearby is known as the material's magnetic field.

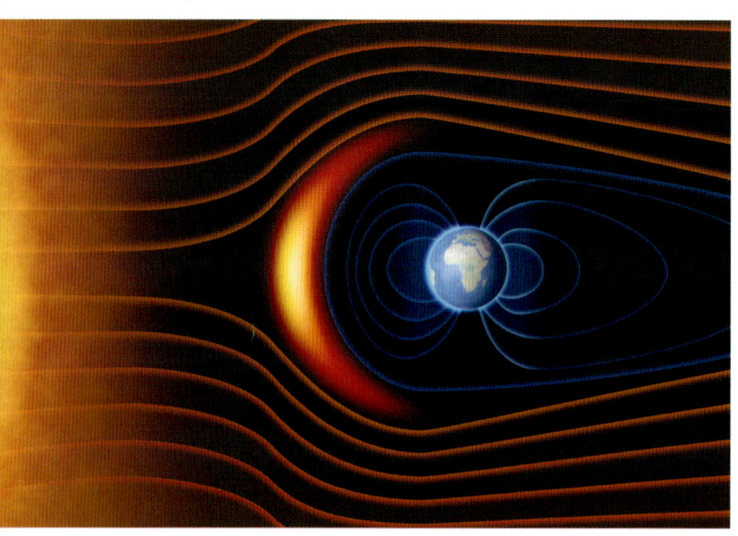

▲ Magnetosphere

Earth as a Magnet

A magnetic compass's needle will point toward the north. While this phenomenon was known for many centuries, nobody knew the exact reason. It was in 1600 that an English scholar, William Gilbert, came up with an explanation.

When his work *De Magnete* was published, it was not only one of the first scientific books published in English, but also the first to describe Earth as a giant magnet. Later analysis did reveal that the Earth acted as a magnet, as it had many molten rocks rich in the magnetic material iron. Like a bar magnet, the Earth's magnetic field stretches out into space. This region is known as the magnetosphere and extends for tens of thousands of kilometres beyond the ionosphere layer of Earth's atmosphere.

The magnetosphere plays a crucial role in protecting the Earth from cosmic rays, ultraviolet radiation, and highly charged particles coming from the Sun and outer space, which would otherwise leach away Earth's upper atmosphere and ozone.

The Earth's magnetic field extends all the way from the planet's interior into space and is also known as the geomagnetic field. The field is created by electric currents caused by the motion of molten iron in the Earth's outer core and the escape of heat from the core.

The north and south magnetic poles of Earth, even though located near the geographic poles, tend to vary across geological time scales. Since the change occurs very slowly, magnetic compasses will remain accurate for navigation. Every few hundred thousand years, the Earth's magnetic field reverses completely.

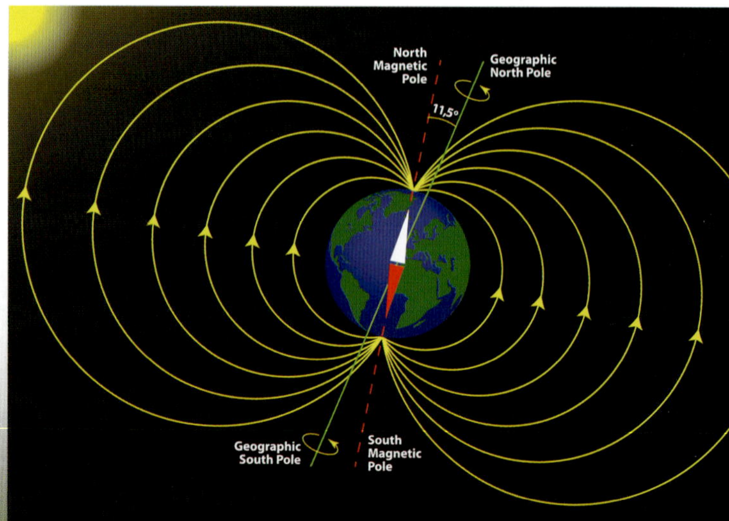

▲ Earth's magnetic field

▲ Neutron star with a powerful magnetic field

The northern lights (aurora borealis) and southern lights (aurora australis) are formed by charged particles in the solar wind interacting with Earth's magnetic field.

Strength of Magnetic Field

A magnet's magnetic field strength is strongest close to the magnet and decreases with distance. The strength of the magnetic field is measured in units called teslas and gauss, named after two scientists.

Even though Earth is like a huge magnet, it has a surprisingly weak magnetic field. In fact, Earth's magnetic field is 100–1,000 times weaker than an average bar magnet. The biggest lab magnet on the planet exhibits a magnetic field that is 900,000 times stronger than that of Earth!

The Sun has a magnetic field many times stronger than the Earth's. Jupiter, Saturn, Uranus, and Neptune also have magnetic fields stronger than that of Earth. However, Mercury, Venus and Mars have magnetic fields much weaker than Earth's. Our Moon does not exhibit any magnetism.

Neutron stars are small but dense and collapsed cores of large stars. They have the most powerful magnetic fields known in the universe, in the range of 104–1,011 teslas. To give a comparison, the highest magnetic field that has been generated in the laboratory is 16 teslas, enough to lift up a live frog.

Magnetic Materials

Magnets are not only interesting objects to play and experiment with; they are important components of appliances and technology we use every day. Different materials exhibit different degrees of magnetism.

▲ Magnets

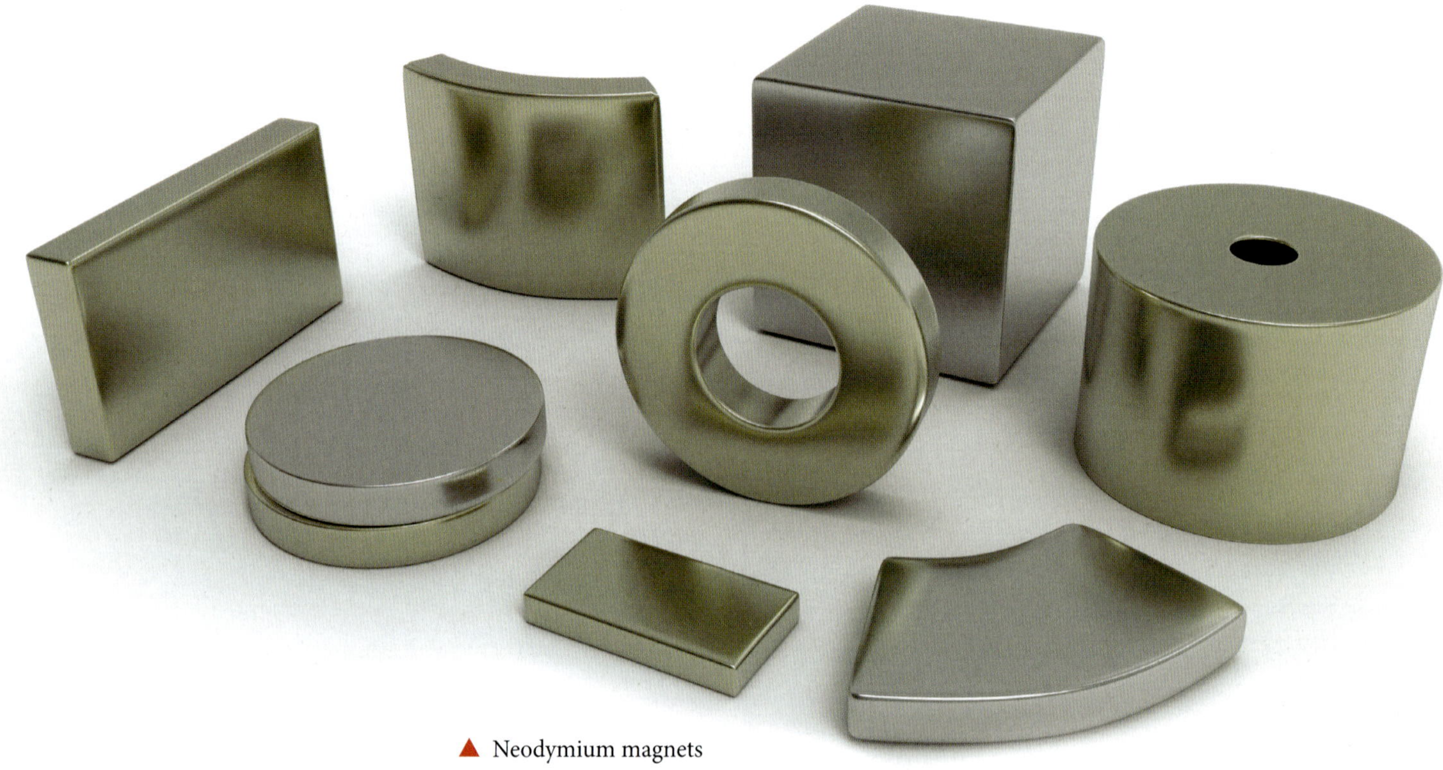

▲ Neodymium magnets

Magnetic and Nonmagnetic Materials

When one thinks of magnets, iron is the first metal to come to mind. Iron exhibits strong magnetism. Other elements within the periodic table that also exhibit magnetism include some rare earth metals such as nickel, cobalt, samarium, and neodymium.

Ferrites are compounds made of iron, oxygen, and other elements and exhibit good magnetism. Lodestone, which is known as magnetite, is an example of a naturally occurring ferrite compound that was initially discovered and used by people in ancient times.

Other metals like copper, aluminium, gold, and silver do not exhibit magnetism. Materials like wood, rubber, plastic, concrete, paper, glass, wool, and cloth fibres do not exhibit magnetism either.

▲ Magnetic materials

Properties of Magnetic Materials

Even though iron is strongly magnetic, it is useful only as a temporary magnet, because it exhibits magnetism only when a magnet is brought near an iron object. Such a material is said to be 'magnetically soft.' On the other hand, iron alloys and rare earth metals retain their magnetic properties even when they are removed from the magnetic field of another magnet. Such a material is said to be 'magnetically hard.' The extent to which a material can be magnetized is known as its susceptibility.

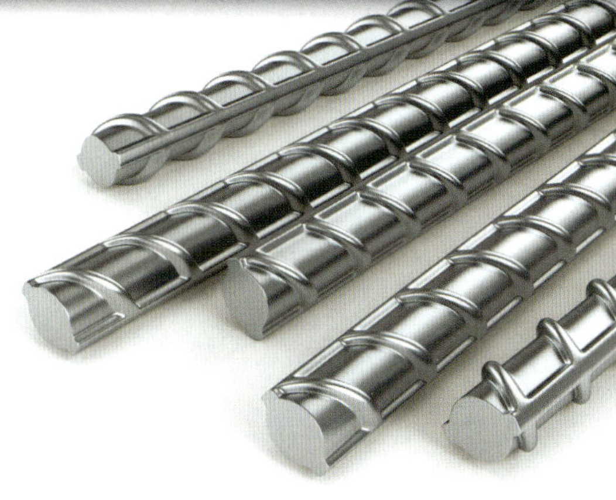
▲ Steel bars

Types of Magnetic Materials

All known materials on Earth can be divided into one of three categories based on their magnetic properties: paramagnetic ferromagnetic and diamagnetic.

1) Paramagnetic: A material, that, when hung from a thread, is capable of magnetising itself and aligning parallel to the Earth's magnetic field, is said to be paramagnetic. Certain metals like aluminium and even many non-metals are paramagnetic. The magnetism they exhibit is so weak that it is barely noticeable. Paramagnetic property is influenced by temperature—the hotter a paramagnetic material is, the less likely it is to respond to magnets placed close to it.

▲ Styrofoam is a diamagnetic material.

2) Ferromagnetic: Iron and a few other materials such as the rare earth metals become strongly magnetized in the presence of a magnetic field and have the ability to remain magnetized even after the magnetic field is removed. Such materials are said to be ferromagnetic. The word 'ferromagnetic' means 'magnetic like iron.' Ferromagnetic materials will lose their magnetism when they are heated above a certain temperature. This temperature is variable and known as the Curie temperature. For example, iron has a Curie temperature of 770°C, while nickel's Curie temperature is 800°C. Heating an iron magnet above its Curie temperature or repeatedly hitting it can weaken or destroy its ferromagnetic properties.

3) Diamagnetic: While ferromagnetic and paramagnetic materials respond positively to magnetism, there are others that resist magnetisation. Such materials are said to be diamagnetic. Water and many carbon compounds are diamagnetic in nature. When a diamagnetic material is suspended on a string, it will align at an angle of 180 degrees to the Earth's magnetic field.

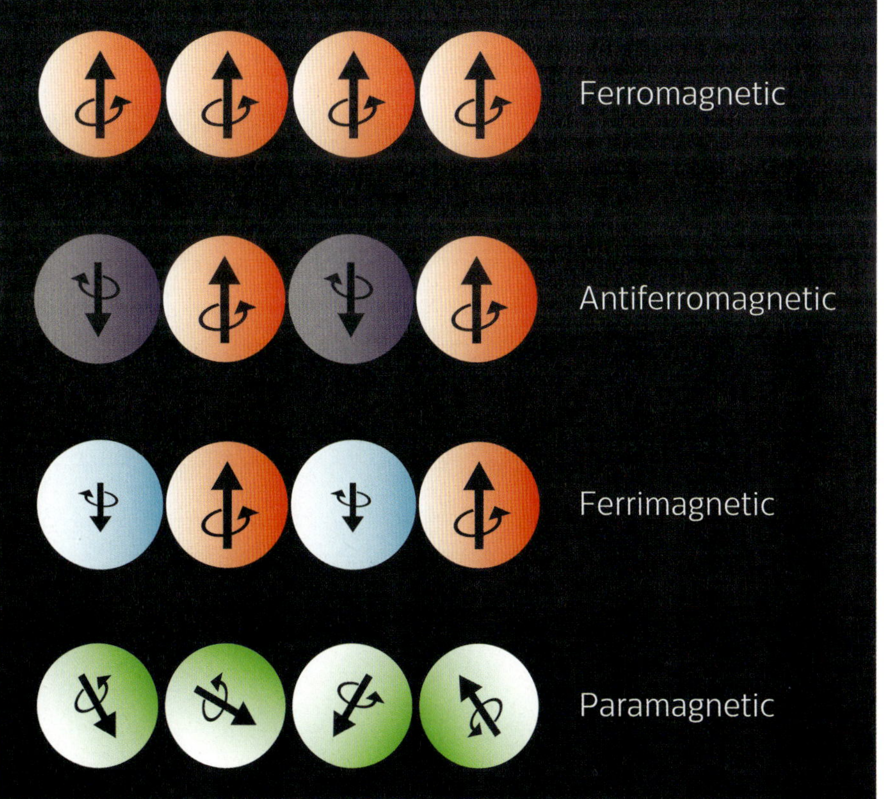

Magnetic Levitation

The use of magnetic fields to levitate or lift a mostly metallic object is known as magnetic levitation. In this process, the suspended object is supported only by magnetic fields. This technology is also sometimes referred to as 'electromagnetic suspension.'

Magnetic Levitation Principle

In magnetic levitation, electromagnetism is employed as a force to counteract gravity. However, levitation cannot be achieved by generating a simple electromagnetic field. A superconductor is used for making levitation viable and safe. A superconductor is a diamagnetic material that repels a magnetic field. This method of magnetic levitation is also known as 'electrodynamic propulsion.'

Maglev Trains

At present, with congested airports and frequent delays, people look for options other than flights to travel from one location to another. All other modes of transport apart from airplanes are too slow by today's standards. Scientists have devised a new and revolutionary alternative to air travel—maglev trains. A few countries have already developed high-speed maglev trains and operate them using powerful electromagnets.

Maglev (magnetic levitation) trains are designed to be suspended in air above the track and propelled forward to their destinations purely through magnetism. Since the trains are not directly in contact with the track, there is no friction except between the train carriages and the air. As a result, maglev trains can travel at very high speeds, up to about 500 to 650 kilometres/hour. Better still, these trains can run at low noise levels and only consume relatively small amounts of energy.

◀ Maglev train

Maglev Trains and Conventional Trains

The maglev train differs considerably from a conventional train in more than one aspect. Maglev trains are not equipped with typical engines that are used for pulling carriages along the tracks. Maglev trains do not run on fossil fuels and instead are powered by the electrified coils of wire present in the track walls which propel them forward.

Maglev Train Operation

Maglev trains operate through three main components:

1) Large electrical power source

2) Metal coils lining a track

3) Large magnets attached to the underside of the train for guiding it along the track

The magnetized coils running along the track repel the large magnets present under the train.

Once the train is levitated, it receives power from the coils in the track walls to generate a system of magnetic fields to pull or push the train along the track.

The alternating current supplied to the coils is constantly altering so as to change the polarity of the magnetized coils. This change in polarity causes the magnetic field in front of the train to guide it forward.

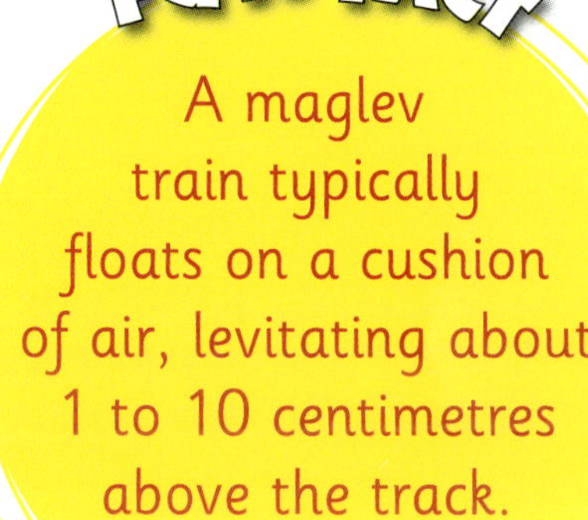

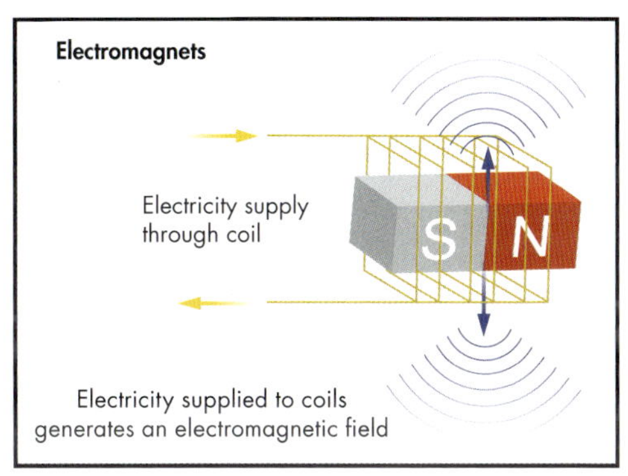
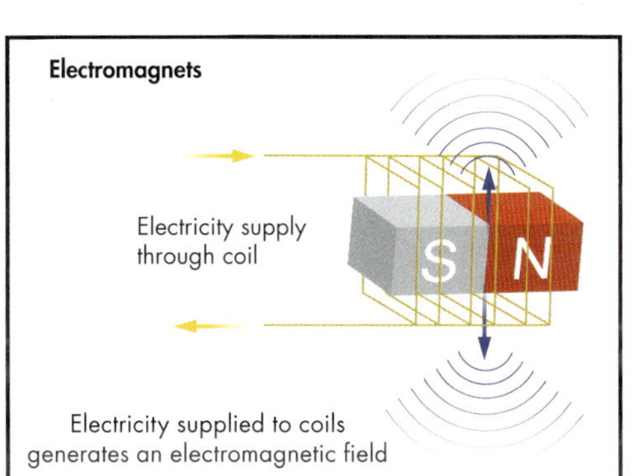
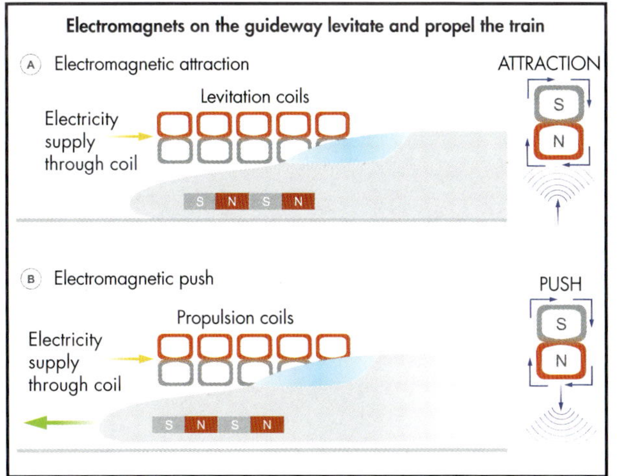

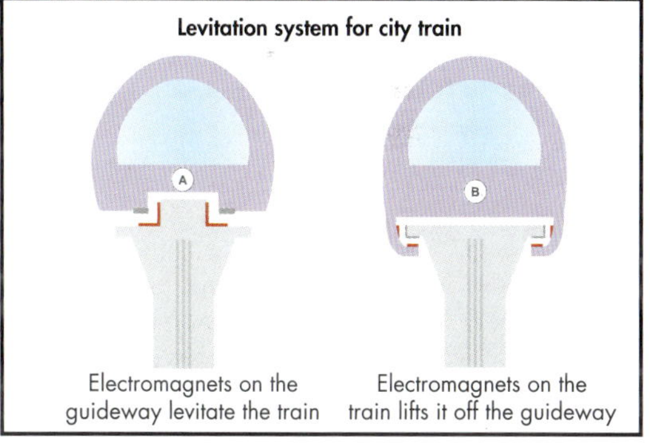
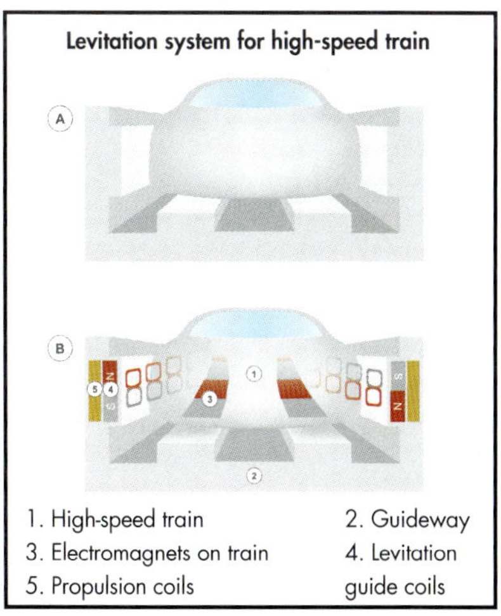

▲ Magnetic levitation mechanism

Electromagnetic Radiation

Electromagnetic (EM) radiation refers to a form of energy that we find everywhere around us. It can travel without any medium, unlike sound or vibrations, which need a medium for transmission. It is the energy emanated through the oscillation of a combination of electric and magnetic fields.

Discovery of EM Radiation

James Clerk Maxwell became the first scientist to suggest the existence of electromagnetic waves. He not only developed a scientific theory to describe EM radiation but also derived equations to describe the relation between the electric and magnetic fields. Maxwell's theory was later successfully applied to the generation of electromagnetic waves by another scientist, Heinrich Hertz.

▲ James Clerk Maxwell

▲ Electromagnetic wave

Properties of EM Radiation

Electromagnetic radiation is energy emitted radially through the combined vibrations of electrical and magnetic fields. Electromagnetic radiation has a dual nature—depending on the circumstances, it can act as a wave or particles. When EM radiation is treated as a wave, it will possess velocity, wavelength, and frequency. As particles, it is referred to as photons.

The electric and magnetic fields that make up an electromagnetic wave are perpendicular to each other along the direction in which it is travelling. EM radiation usually travels at the speed of light until it comes in contact with matter that can interfere with its propagation, such as a block of metal or water.

Generally, electromagnetic radiation is classified by wavelength into radio waves, microwaves, visible light (ranging from ultraviolet to the infrared range), X-rays, and high-energy gamma rays.

The electromagnetic radiation classification is based on three main properties:

1) **Energy:** The energy of EM radiation is its intensity and is expressed in electron volts. Energy is calculated especially while measuring high-energy radiation like X-rays or gamma rays.

2) **Wavelength**: The wavelength of EM radiation is the measure of the distance between the wave repetitions. The wavelength is useful for describing the shape and movement of the wave.

3) **Frequency:** Frequency of an EM wave is the number of crests (maximum upward rise of a wave) and troughs (maximum downward point of a wave) passing through a point in any given second.

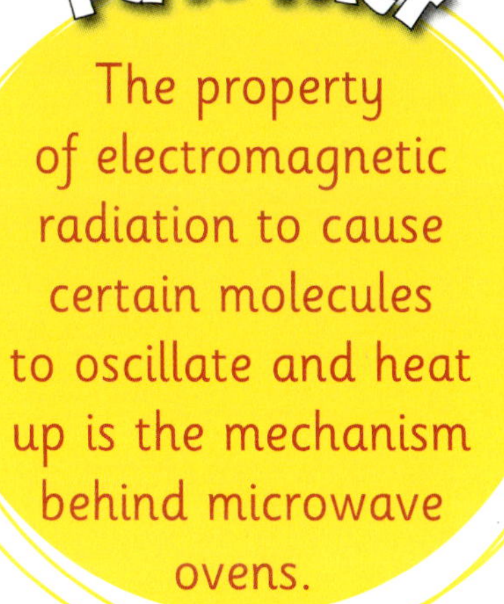

FUN FACT

The property of electromagnetic radiation to cause certain molecules to oscillate and heat up is the mechanism behind microwave ovens.

ELECTROMAGNETIC SPECTRUM

Electromagnetic Spectrum

The electromagnetic spectrum refers to the range of frequencies of electromagnetic radiation of different wavelengths and energies. This frequency range is divided into bands ranging from radio waves, microwaves, infrared, visible light, ultraviolet, X-rays, and gamma rays. Among them, ultraviolet radiation, X-rays, and gamma rays are referred to as 'ionising radiation.'

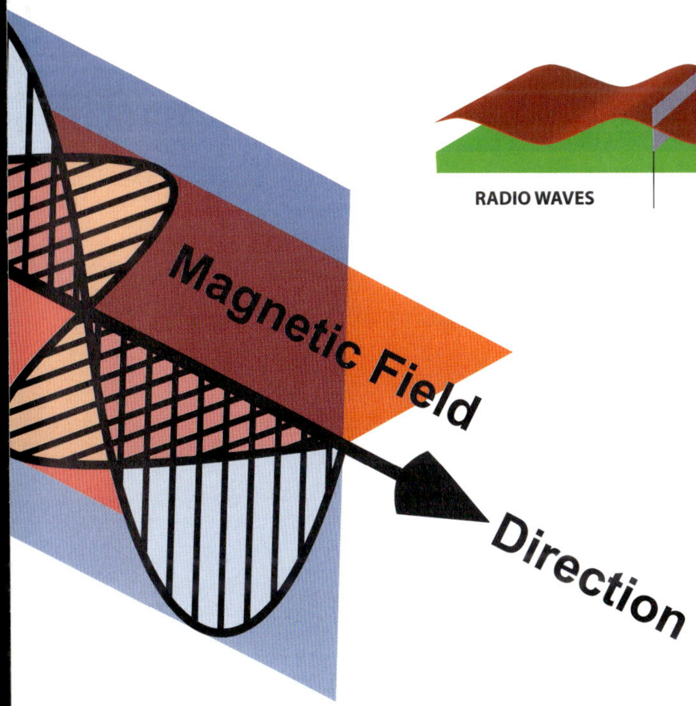

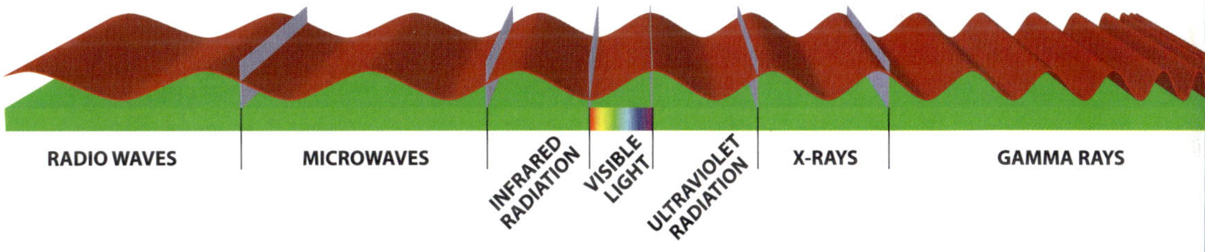

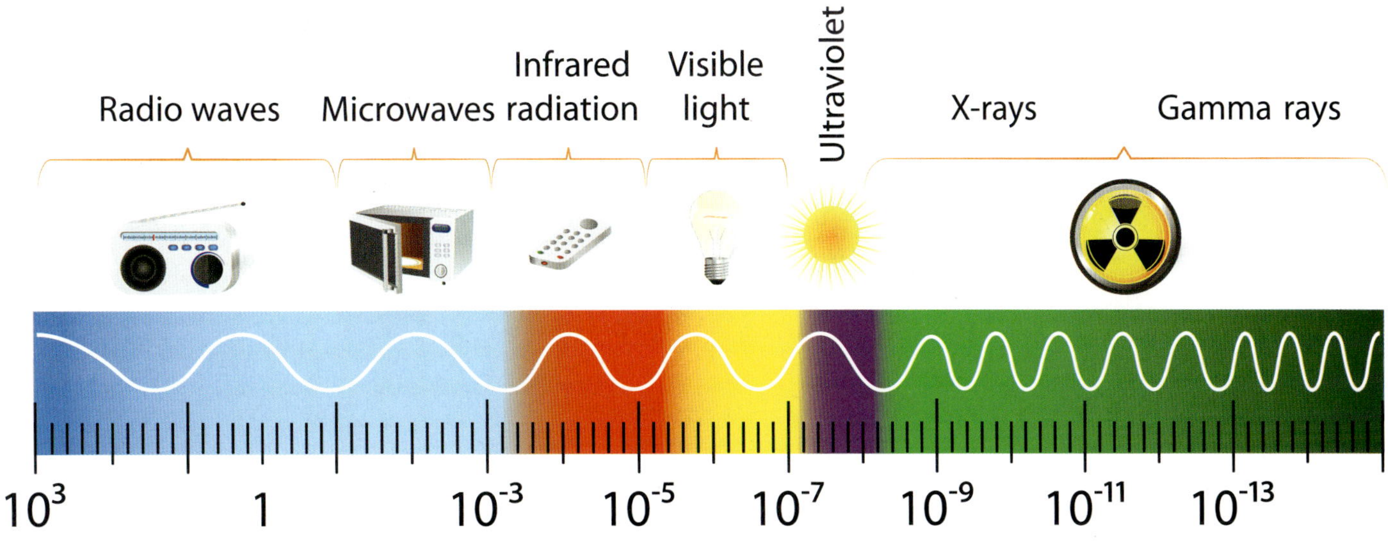

Electromagnetism

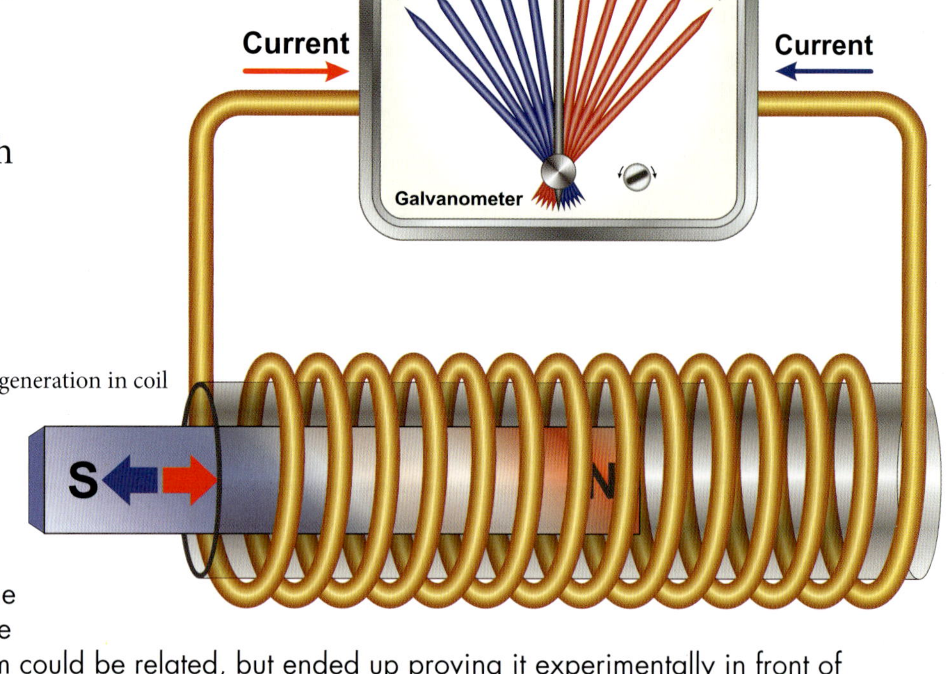

When the relationship between electricity and magnetism was identified, it led to a new branch of study and the development of many essential applications that we use every day in the modern world.

▶ Magnet and current generation in coil

Discovery of Electromagnetism

Hans Christian Oersted discovered the phenomenon of electromagnetism quite by accident in 1820 when he was in the midst of a lecture. He had suggested the possibility that electricity and magnetism could be related, but ended up proving it experimentally in front of his students. He passed electric current through a metallic wire and when a magnetic compass was suspended above it, the needle moved in response to the current.

▲ Electricity and magnetism relationship

Electromagnetic Properties

Electrons flowing through a conductor result in the formation of a magnetic field around the conducting material. The magnetic field lines will always be oriented perpendicularly to the direction of the flow of electricity.

The magnetic field produced by an electric wire can be increased by winding the wire into tight coils instead of stretching it out in a straight line. The magnetic field force produced by an electromagnet is called the magnetomotive force. This force is proportional to the product of current passing through the electromagnet and the number of coils in the wire.

The property of electromagnetism is extensively applied to many research, medical, industrial, and daily purposes. One of the very first uses of an electromagnet was to power mechanical devices to produce mechanical force from electricity. The electric motor is the best example of one of the first applications of electromagnets.

Electromagnetic Induction

Just as the movement of electric current in a wire can generate a magnetic field, the movement of an electric wire through a magnetic field within a magnet will generate an electric current.

Fleming's left-hand rule is used for electric motors, while Fleming's right-hand rule is used for electric generators. We already have a magnetic field and motion of a wire through that field, so to calculate the direction of current induced, we use the right-hand rule.

With the three fingers of the right hand at right angles to each other, the thumb represents the direction of motion, the first finger the direction of the magnetic field, and the second finger the direction of the induced current.

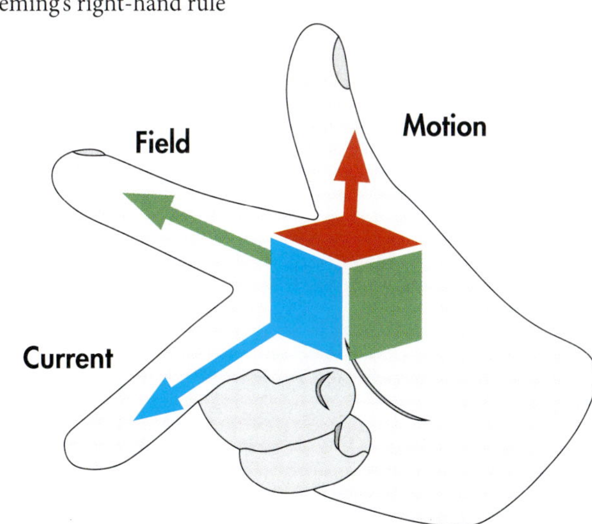

Direction of current for generators, using Fleming's right-hand rule

An MRI machine uses a superconducting electromagnet.

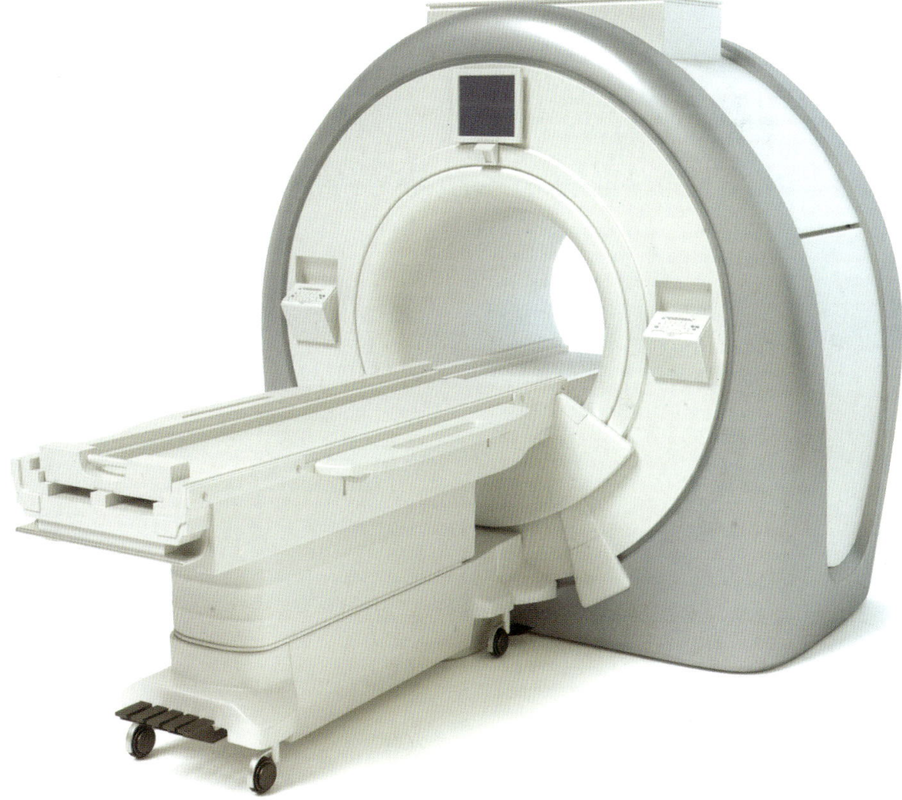

Electromagnets, designed for different purposes, can be of any of the three types:

1) Resistive: A resistive electromagnet uses copper wires or copper plates to generate magnetic fields. A magnetic field can be concentrated by twisting the wire around a piece of metal.

2) Superconducting: This type of electromagnet operates by reducing electrical resistance. It operates in very cold temperatures and can continue functioning even after the power supply is turned off.

3) Hybrid: This type of electromagnet is made by combining resistive and superconducting electromagnets.

Electromagnets

Today, scientists have identified that electromagnetism is one of the fundamental forces operating across the universe. It is responsible for electricity, magnetism, and light. Starting with the demonstration of electromagnetism at the lab level, today it has become a regular feature in many devices and industrial processes we use.

▶ Hans Christian Oersted

History

Electromagnets came into existence following the breakthrough discovery by the Danish scientist Hans Christian Oersted. When a battery was turned on, the electric wire deflected the magnetic needle, leading him to propose that the electric wire radiated magnetic fields from all sides.

Oersted published his findings and mathematically proved that the current flowing through a wire produced a magnetic field. In 1824, about four years later, an English scientist, William Sturgeon, developed the first electromagnet.

▲ Electric field in the presence of magnet

It was a horseshoe-shaped piece of iron wrapped tightly with copper wire. When current was passed through the wire, it attracted other pieces of iron scraps, but when the current supply was cut off, it lost its magnetisation property. By modern standards, the electromagnet designed by Sturgeon was too weak to be useful for any practical purpose. However, weighing about 200 grams, it was capable of lifting weights up to 9 pounds.

Later, in the 1930s, the American scientist Joseph Henry made many improvements in the basic design of the electromagnet to improve its efficiency. He used insulated wire and placed thousands of turns of wire on a single core. His electromagnet was so effective that it was capable of lifting and supporting weights of about 2,000 lbs. Joseph Henry's revolutionary design modification made electromagnets popular and paved the way for innovations and uses for scientific, industrial, and practical purposes.

Working of an Electromagnet

An electromagnet is a piece of wire that is designed to generate a strong magnetic field when electric current is passed through it. All conducting materials and current-carrying wires generate a magnetic field, but an electromagnet is specially designed to maximize the strength of the magnetic field.

It is possible to construct a simple electromagnet at home by taking an iron nail and wrapping it tightly with copper wires in many coils and connecting the two ends to a battery. This 'electromagnet' is now capable of attracting small metal clips or iron filings.

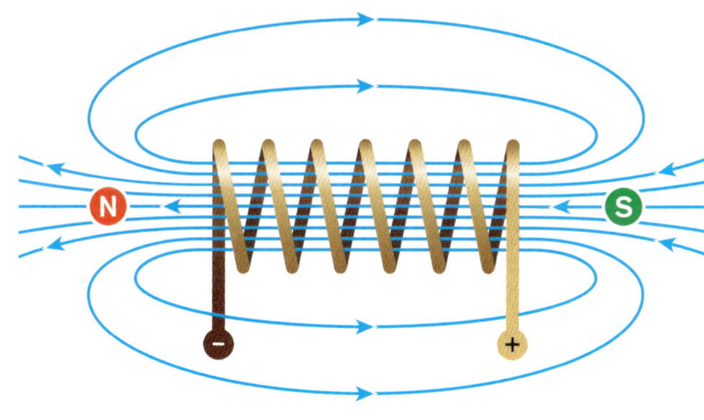

▲ Electromagnetism

Permanent Magnets and Electromagnets

A permanent magnet has fixed north and south poles that cannot be altered or artificially fixed. In an electromagnet, the north and south polarity can be altered simply by changing the direction of electric current applied to a coil. A permanent magnet's magnetic field strength cannot be altered. An electromagnet's strength can be altered by changing the current flowing through the coil or by reducing or increasing the number of coils.

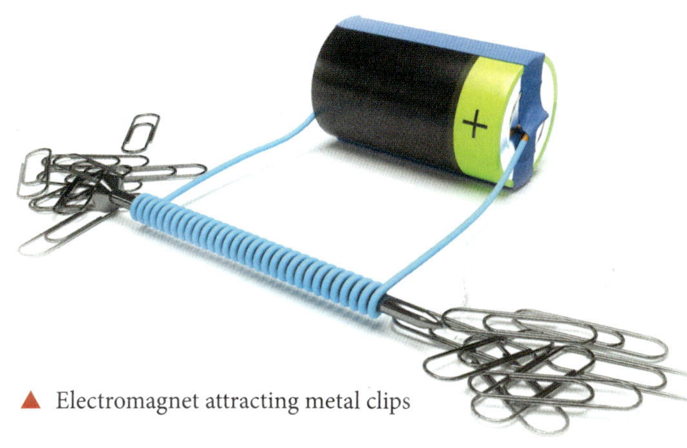

▲ Electromagnet attracting metal clips

FUN FACT

Only a naturally magnetic material like iron, nickel, or cobalt (or a mixture of magnetic materials) can be used to make an electromagnet.

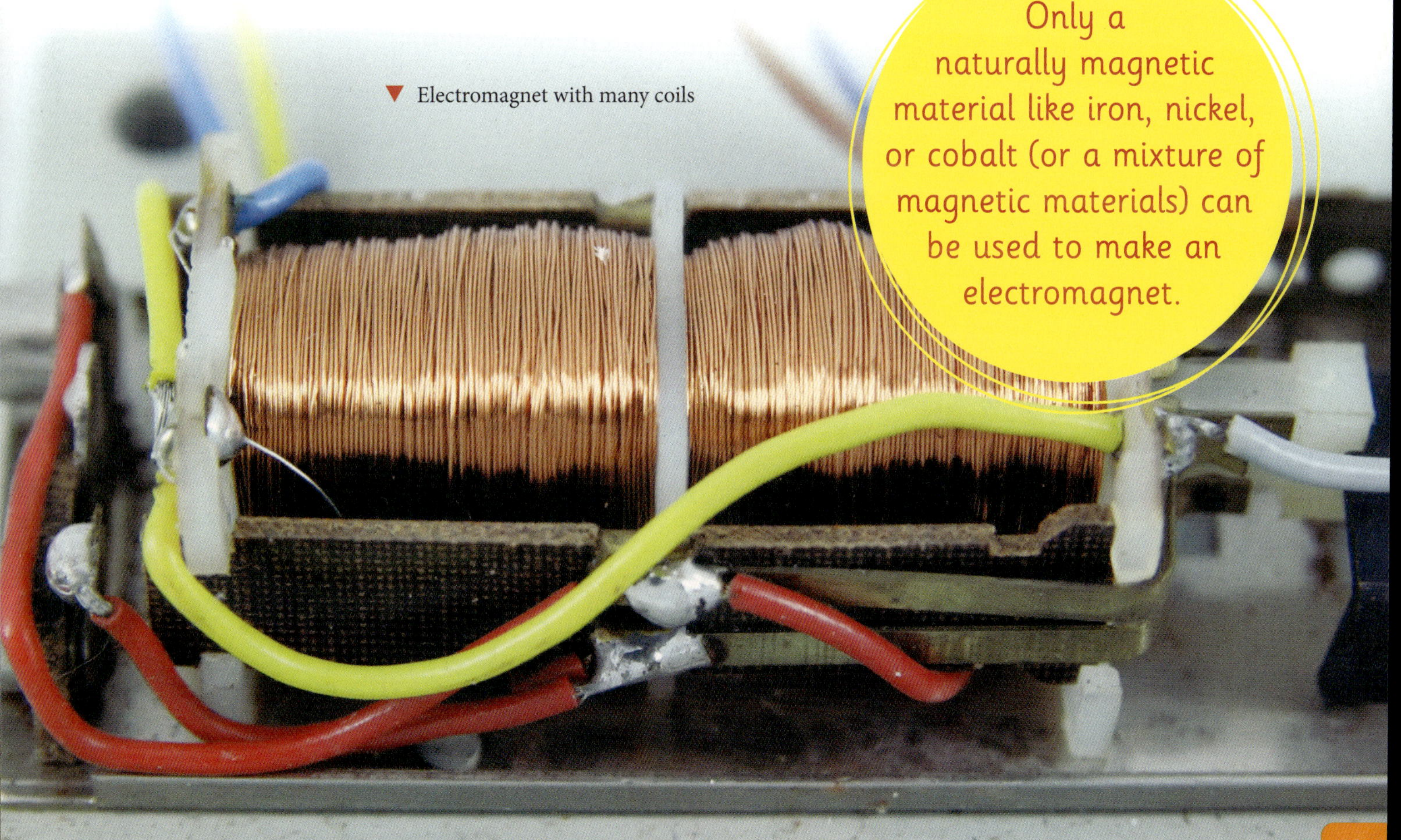

▼ Electromagnet with many coils

Applications of Electromagnetism and EM Radiation

Electromagnetism and EM radiation serve many useful purposes. Today, many practical everyday applications as well as research depend largely on the direct or indirect employment of electromagnets or electromagnetic radiation.

▼ Large Hadron Collider

Uses of Electromagnetism

Ranging from minute electronic components to large-scale industrial machines, electromagnetism has many important applications. It is also used in research and experimentation purposes in many fields of science. Electromagnets offer an advantage over conventional magnets in that they can be controlled by switching the electricity on or off.

1. A solenoid is a type of electromagnet that is used in pinball machines, dot matrix printers, and paintball markers. All these devices require that magnetism be applied and controlled precisely for organized movement of certain components.

2. Superconducting electromagnets are used in scientific and research equipment such as nuclear magnetic resonance (NMR) spectrometers, mass spectrometers, and particle accelerators. The Large Hadron Collider (LHC) is an example of a massive particle accelerator.

3. Electromagnets are used in musical and sound equipment, including loudspeakers, earphones, and electric bells, and in magnetic recording and data storage in the form of tape recorders.

4. Electromagnets are also used in the multimedia and entertainment industry to create devices and components like data recorders and hard discs.

5. Electric actuators are motors used for converting electrical energy to mechanical energy, and use electromagnets to achieve this.

6. Power transformers function by increasing or decreasing voltage of alternating current transmitted along power lines. Electromagnetic induction is the principle behind the function of power transformation.

7. Induction cooking that uses electricity for heating and cooking food uses electromagnets.

8. Magnetic separators that sort and lift ferromagnetic material from scraps in the junkyard also use electromagnets.

9. MRI machines used for medical imaging and diagnosis employ electromagnets.

Uses of EM Radiation

EM radiation plays an important role in our everyday lives. Among the many applications, listed below are a few:

1. EM radiation in the form of long- and short-wavelength radio waves is used in broadcasting radio programs.

2. It is used widely in communication technology for transmitting TV, telephone, and wireless signals.

3. EM radiation is used in radars (radio sensing) for guiding and remote sensing for studying Earth's features.

4. Ultraviolet radiation is used in sterilisation purposes for killing microbes and germs. It is also used for detecting forged bank notes.

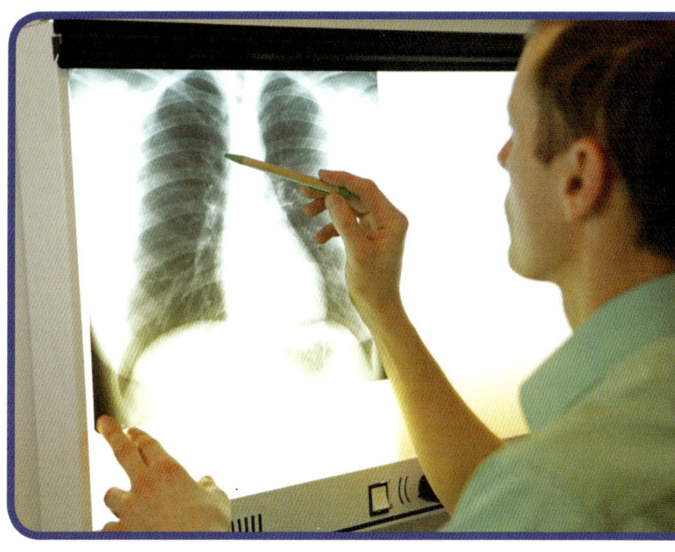

▲ Medical application of X-rays

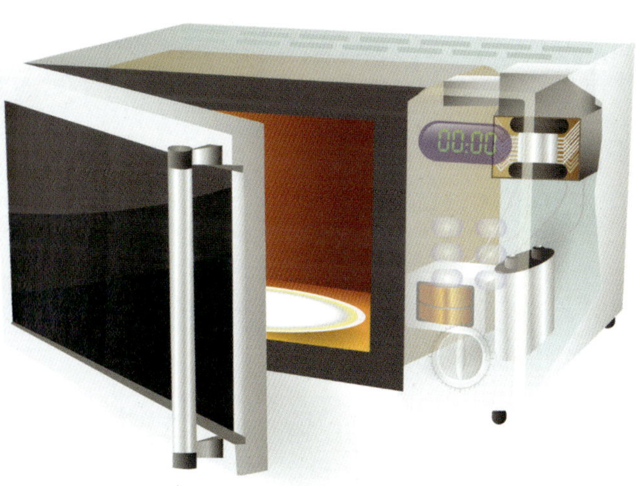

▲ Microwave oven

5. X-rays can pass through the flesh and are used in detecting fractures or joint dislocations inside the body, and in general medical diagnosis.

6. Gamma rays are highly charged particles that can cause cancer upon exposure. However, they are also useful for killing cancer cells when used at the right levels.

7. Infrared radiation is used for night-vision devices and security cameras and is employed extensively by military forces across the world.

8. Microwaves are used for heating and cooking, employed in microwave oven technology. They are also used for satellite signals, as microwave radiation is capable of passing through clouds and atmosphere.

◀ Satellites capture radio wave signals.

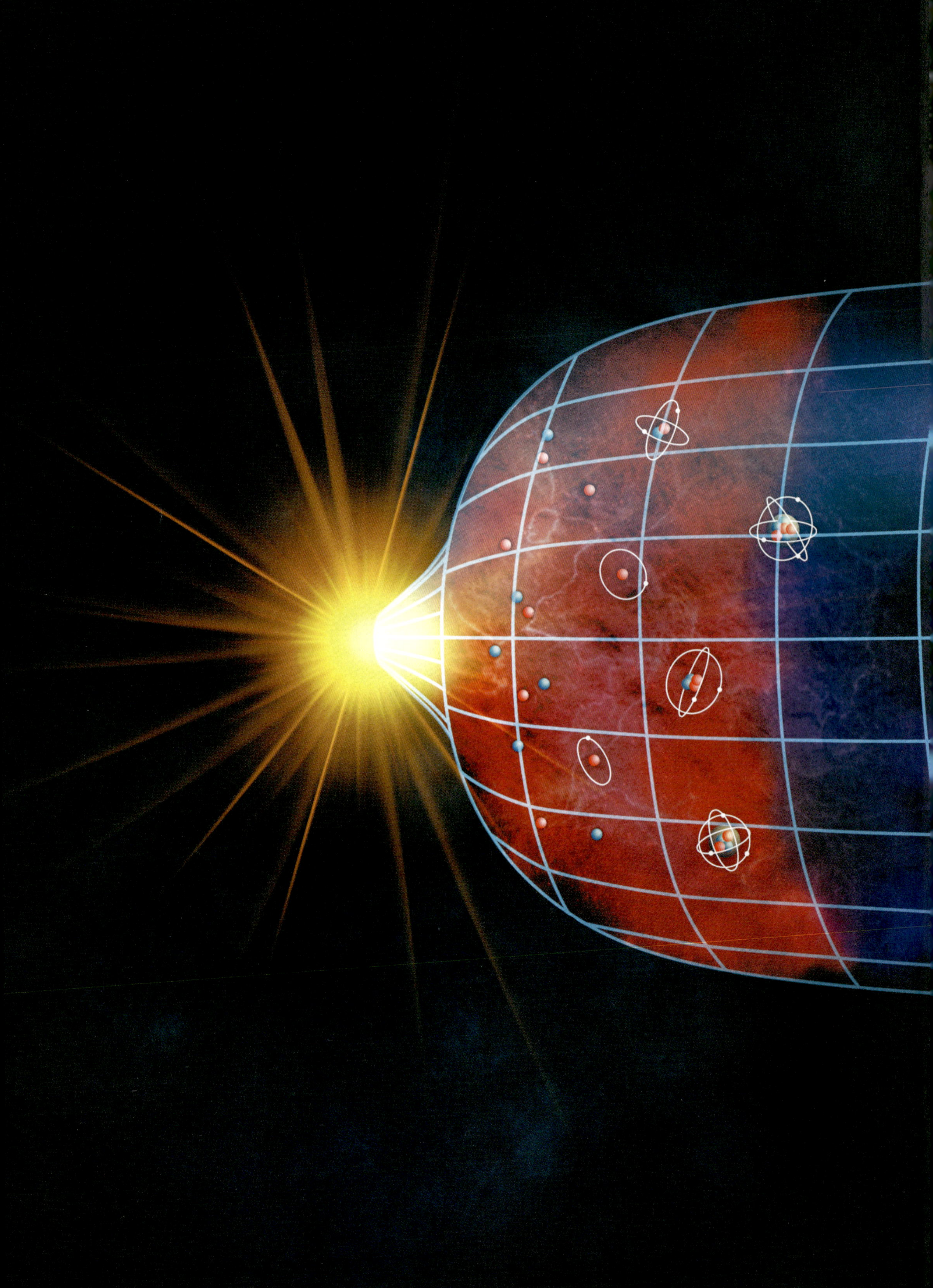